TRAVEL JAPAN

UNVEILING CULTURE, LANGUAGE & LOCAL GEMS

P.D. MASON

Copyright © 2023 - P.D. Mason - SugarDog Publishing - All Rights Reserved.

The content created within this book may not be reproduced, duplicated, or transmitted without direct written permission from the author or the publisher.

Under no circumstances will any blame or legal responsibility be held against the publisher or author for any damages, reparation, or monetary loss due to the information contained within this book, either directly or indirectly.

Legal Notice:

This book is copyright-protected. It is only for personal use. You may not amend, distribute, sell, use, quote, or paraphrase any part of this publication without the author's and publisher's express consent.

Disclaimer Notice:

Please be advised that the information contained in this book is for educational and entertainment purposes only. All efforts have been executed to present accurate, up-to-date, reliable, and complete information.

No warranties of any kind are declared or implied, Readers understand, acknowledge, and agree that the author is not engaged in the rendering of legal, financial, medical, or professional advice.

The content within this book has been derived from various sources. Please consult a licensed professional before attempting any techniques outlined in this book.

Cover Photo Notice:

Cover photo used with written permission from Olson, Brian P. (Japan snapshot at Fushimi Inari-Taisha). *Travel Japan: Unveiling Culture, Language & Local Gems*, P.D. Mason, SugarDog Publishing, 2023, Front Cover.

CONTENTS

Introduction   v

1. Planning Your Trip to Japan   1
2. Five Amazing Cities   15
3. Arriving By Air   33
4. Understanding the Rail System   45
5. Dining Japanese Style   53
6. Lodging In Japan   65
7. Weather In The Five Cities   73
8. Top Attractions   85
9. The Snowy Wonderland of Japan   99
10. Final Thoughts   113

About the Author   117
Also by P.D. Mason   118
References   119

INTRODUCTION

WELCOME!

Greetings readers! If you're at any stage of your travel planning for a whirlwind trip of a lifetime to Japan, you've bought the right book! The first thing I will tell you is this book is not filled with loads of colorful snapshots taken at various Japanese tourist attractions used in a manner to entice you to travel to Japan. I assume since you've decided to read this book, you are in some stage of planning your trip, whether it's just an idea or you've started to do some research.

This book should be used as your research tool and your research reference. You should mark this book with thoughts and notes you can easily reference while traversing Japan by rail, car, or foot. If that sounds like a bright idea, it's only because our travel party had multiple books we carried in our luggage, and many of them had little sticky flags (like the "Sign Here" flags you'd see on an important document). The problem with the travel books we traveled with was that they were large —hundreds and hundreds of pages, and heavy.

On foot in Japan, the weight of luggage or backpacks is everything. We spent hours on trains and waiting for trains or making connections through multiple train stations, and with a heavy pack on my back, I often wished I could re-distribute the contents of my pack right there on the train platform. We walked and walked and walked some more. It was VERY well worth every step we took. I believe an app on my phone indicated we had walked nearly 85 miles (136km) in the eleven days of our trip, and even shedding just one of those travel books would have been a dream.

This book is compact and small enough to fit nicely in your luggage and is small enough to be used when there are questions or a quick look up of something in the book is needed. We hope you find this reference guide extremely useful as we've loaded it with the most pertinent "convenience" factors.

My wife and I started our Japan planning sessions early in 2021, about six months after our child arrived in Japan for a three-year posting at a military base. Sometime thereafter, the Coronavirus pandemic hit in full force, squashing any hope of visiting this beautiful country until the Japanese government opened tourism again within its borders.

We had plenty of time to craft our itinerary through many hours of discussion about the parts of Japan we'd like to visit. We relied on our military child to provide us with the must-sees and the must-dos in Japan, as our child has had multiple short-excursion experiences in Tokyo and could at least give us some starting-point details. Additionally, we relied heavily on social media posts in a prevalent Japan Travel Facebook group, which helped us narrow down our itinerary based on the time of year we intended to travel.

Multiple video conferencing calls with the enlisted child formed a plan for our travel party of seven with the number of days we'd need to experience what we wanted, and the rest just fell into place.

Our travel journey in Japan was eleven days, including the days on the front and back ends for travel from the Midwest, USA. However, I did factor in the travel days we'd have in Japan as the time zone difference, and the crossing of the international date line didn't affect us too much with the loss of travel time for our trip.

Based on the military child's suggestion, we devised our itinerary, which landed us in Tokyo and ultimately would take us as far as 500 miles (805km) from Tokyo to Hiroshima. We now had a base to work around, and the research began to fill in the middle.

Ultimately, we knew that we wanted a trip to Japan that would bring us to the biggest and best attractions that would likely be impactful enough to warrant the yearning for a return trip, and we hit that nail on the head.

Our itinerary covered four significant cities, Tokyo, Kyoto, Osaka, and Hiroshima, and also covered a lesser-known town that was by far a highlight of the trip, Kamakura, which is a Pacific Ocean seaside coastal town that could have been easily mistaken for any US Eastern seaboard coastal town. Although Kamakura is a town that heavily relies on tourism, the sheer quaint feel of the town as one meanders through is appreciated by tourists and natives alike.

This book will give you what I consider to be the biggest and the best attractions in each of the five cities we visited. Along the way, I'll interject why we chose the cities in the order we did and why we decided to see the sights we did while passing on other tourist attractions.

This is a "budget-friendly" itinerary, so the book's title eludes to a spend-thrifty mentality. This book does not lead the reader into a dollar amount a person or a family should budget for travel within Japan, as every person and family has a different idea of what an acceptable budget will be for themselves or their families.

Airfare to Japan from the US is costly by any means. Still, for a once-in-a-lifetime chance of a trip, my partner and I knew it was what it was – and we weren't going to pass on the opportunity to visit the country where our child had been delegated to spend three years performing his military job.

Our trip randomly had a final layout as it did, meaning the cities we chose to stay in, although they had a small amount of thought put into them, and it seemed the correct order as the trip is now behind us.

Tokyo should always be the "jumping off point" for all travelers to Japan, as the Tokyo, Japan International Airport (Haneda Airport) is the landing airport for all major international flights worldwide. Haneda Airport is a sight to be had based on its sheer size, and the layout and general flow of the airport have been very craftily thought out.

From our starting point in Tokyo, we understood that some of our travel itineraries required us to travel over 500 miles (800km) westward from Japan, and that was our basis for determining in which order we would visit the cities. Given that we knew we had a multi-hour Japan Rail train ride from Tokyo to our must-see destination of Hiroshima, we planned this day trip early in our itinerary as it would be an early morning to possibly late night trip.

The remaining cities we wanted to visit, Kyoto, Osaka, and Kamakura, are all rich in Japanese history throughout the reign of the Japanese Empires and the Shoguns, who were the perceived military leaders of their time, in addition to the ever-present modern-day Buddhist temples that have some of the most interesting construction methods ever seen from hundreds of years ago.

Each city we visited was highly regarded when we were doing our research, so by no means do I claim to be an expert at creating a travel itinerary, as I just followed recommendations from hours of research and our child's recommendations based on things learned while stationed in Japan. For our known travel days and our total allocation of days spent within Japan, we just knew that we were packing as much as humanly possible into our nine whole days and a travel day at each end of our trip of a lifetime.

What works for one might only sometimes work for another, so I am giving you the details of our itinerary with a caveat: it may not work for you, and you may find that you need to allocate more time to your Japan visit.

Based on the schedule of our military child, we knew we'd have enough time to complete what we set out to do – and that got just a fraction of a taste of what life in Japan is like, based on the cities we visited and the sights and attractions we took in.

As I said, our itinerary may not work precisely for you as it did for us, and that's ok. We want to provide a baseline of places westward from Tokyo that are well worth their costs to see, and from there, you can derive your itinerary and experience Japan the way you'd most like.

With that, I bid you safe travels and Arigatou gozaimasu for putting trust into this book to help you navigate a beautiful country rich with history and customs dating back centuries.

Again, happy reading, and safe travels on your excursion to Japan!

1

PLANNING YOUR TRIP TO JAPAN

EMBARKING on a journey to Japan is an exciting endeavor that promises a captivating blend of tradition, delicious meals, and cultural immersion. Careful planning and research are essential to ensure a smooth and rewarding experience. This chapter discusses some crucial aspects of planning your trip to Japan, including visa requirements, optimal travel seasons, budgeting, and cultural customs. By equipping yourself with the necessary knowledge, you'll be able to create an itinerary that caters to your interests, navigate the country with ease, and embrace the wonders that Japan has to offer.

> **Importance of research and itinerary planning.** Before setting foot in Japan, conducting thorough research and creating a well-thought-out itinerary is paramount. Japan is a diverse country with abundant attractions, and knowing what interests you most will help you make the most of your time— research popular destinations, historical landmarks, cultural experiences, and local events that align with your preferences. Consider transportation options, travel distances, and language barriers to ensure a seamless journey. One of the most popular

and useful pre-planning items you could do as a traveler is to do an internet search for JNTO, which will bring you to the official tourism guide for Japanese travel. Within this website, you can download many colorful guides loaded with information for nearly all 47 prefectures located within the nine regions of Japan. The Japanese Government sponsors this website and provides this information to tourists.

Visa requirements and necessary documents. Understanding visa requirements and preparing the necessary documents is essential for travelers visiting Japan. Research the visa regulations applicable to your country of residence and ensure that you have a valid passport with sufficient validity. Determine whether you are eligible for a visa waiver program or must apply for a tourist visa in advance. Keep important documents like your passport, travel insurance, and flight itineraries readily accessible throughout your trip.

Best times to visit Japan and considerations for each season. Japan's climate varies across regions, and each season offers a unique experience. Consider the time of year that aligns with your interests and preferences. Spring (March to May) is renowned for its cherry blossoms, while autumn (September to November) dazzles with vibrant foliage. Summer (June to August) offers lively festivals and warm weather, while winter (December to February) showcases stunning snow-covered landscapes. Remember that popular seasons like cherry blossom and autumn foliage attract larger crowds, so plan accordingly.

BUDGETING AND COST ESTIMATION

Budgeting is an essential aspect of trip planning. Japan offers a wide range of options to accommodate various budgets.

Research and estimate the costs of transportation, accommodation, meals, attractions, and activities. Consider staying in budget-friendly accommodations like hostels, guesthouses, or capsule hotels. Enjoy affordable dining options like local eateries, street food, and convenience stores. Research discount passes, like the Japan Rail Pass, that can provide significant transportation savings. Consider additional expenses like entrance fees, souvenirs, and transportation within cities.

Budgeting is crucial when planning a trip to Japan to ensure you make the most of your travel funds. Japan offers a wide range of options that cater to different budgets, allowing you to enjoy the country without breaking the bank. Here are some tips and considerations to help you budget and estimate costs for transportation, accommodation, meals, attractions, and activities:

> **Research and estimate transportation costs.** Transportation in Japan can be efficient but also varied in terms of cost. You should research the different transportation options available, such as trains, buses, and domestic flights, to determine the most suitable and cost-effective choices for your itinerary. If you plan to travel extensively within the country, consider purchasing a Japan Rail Pass, which provides unlimited travel on Japan Railways (JR) lines for a fixed period. This pass can offer significant savings, especially for long-distance travel. For shorter trips, local trains and buses are generally affordable and convenient. A good budget for regular in-city subway trips is two to three dollars per trip from station to station. This excludes Shinkansen (bullet train) fares, as those are covered under a JR Pass. Traveling from one train station to another is very affordable, and that dollar figure I gave you was on the high end of the typical fare.

Consider budget-friendly accommodations. Accommodation costs can vary depending on location and level of comfort. To save money, consider staying in budget-friendly accommodations such as hostels, guesthouses, or capsule hotels. These options offer clean and comfortable facilities at a fraction of the cost of traditional hotels. Additionally, you can explore Japanese-style accommodations like ryokans (traditional inns) for a unique cultural experience. Look for accommodations located slightly outside city centers or in less touristy areas, as they are more affordable.

Explore affordable dining options. Japan is renowned for its culinary delights; you can enjoy delicious meals without breaking your budget. Seek out local eateries, izakayas (Japanese pubs), and street food stalls that offer affordable and flavorful dishes. Convenience stores like FamilyMart and Lawson offer affordable snacks, drinks, and ready-to-eat meals. Take advantage of lunchtime specials or set meal times, which often provide a more cost-effective way to enjoy various Japanese cuisine.

Research attractions and activities. Research the attractions and activities you plan to visit and consider their costs. Many temples, shrines, and parks have modest entrance fees, but some may offer free admission. Prioritize the attractions that align with your interests and budget accordingly. Look out for discounted tickets or combination passes that offer entry to multiple attractions at reduced prices. Additionally, enjoy free activities such as exploring local neighborhoods, attending cultural festivals, or visiting public gardens and parks.

Factor in additional expenses. When budgeting for your trip to Japan, be mindful of additional expenses that may arise. These can include entrance fees for museums, galleries, and theme parks, as well as costs for transportation within cities, such as subway or bus fares. If you plan to purchase souvenirs, allocate a portion of your budget accordingly. To keep track of your expenses, consider using a travel budgeting app or maintaining a spreadsheet to monitor your spending throughout your trip. Additionally, suppose you want to stay "connected" to your smart devices while traveling within Japan. In that case, you'll find information in the book about the options for portable Wi-Fi units that are easy to reserve, pick up, and return at the end of your trip.

Some additional expenses we only discovered would be had once we arrived in the country were things like coffee in the morning and ice cubes if our travel group wanted ice-cold beverages. There are Starbucks coffee shops on nearly every other corner in Tokyo, and if you're anything like our travel party, a few creature comforts of home were well worth the expense. An additional expense we should have factored in before we went was snacks or bottled water while on our day trips. Suppose we had a long day planned of shrines or temples. There comes a point during the day when someone needs a quick energy bar to keep going or bottled water.

Budgeting and cost estimation are essential for planning a successful trip to Japan to ensure no surprises while traveling. By researching and estimating the costs of transportation, accommodation, meals, attractions, and activities, you can make informed decisions that align with your budget. Take advantage of budget-friendly accommodations, explore affordable dining options, and consider discounted passes for transportation and attractions. By planning and being mindful of additional expenses, you can maximize your travel funds and fully immerse yourself in the wonders of Japan without compromising your budget.

JAPAN IS BUILT FOR CONVENIENCE

One of our first stops, usually every morning as we set out for the day, was a convenience store where we could stock up on what we needed. Convenience stores are on nearly every corner of populated cities like Tokyo, Osaka, and Hiroshima. Japan has many convenience stores, such as 7-11, Lawsons, and Family Mart, which are well-supplied with Japanese versions of nearly everything a traveler would need for a day of exploring. From freshly packaged food to native snacks and canned or bottled drinks, whatever is needed for your day trips can be found in these stores.

For more specific items, Don Quijote (pronounced Donkey-hoe-tay) sells everything you can think of, from alcohol to clothing and portable fans to televisions. It's nearly equivalent to a big-box store home store, and they're typically spread out over multiple floors within a building. Don Quijote stores are less prevalent in bigger cities than convenience stores but can be found on a short train ride.

> **Smart Planning Tip #1.** Exchange your currency from your home denomination into Japanese Yen before your departure day. The currency exchange process at our home airport could have been more convenient, and the service charge to make the exchange at the airport was a double-digit percentage fee to make the exchange in addition to a service fee. Most banks in the US provide currency exchange for free as a service to their customers, and it should be as simple as placing the order for the exchange and receiving a phone call a day or two after placing the order, notifying you that the currency is ready for pickup. While traveling in Japan, we noticed many restaurants had small currency counters at the host stand (reminiscent of a US change machine), where you would be greeted upon entry.

It was only clear what the machines were placed there for once a charming restaurant employee pointed to the machine after a meal when we were trying to offload a pocketful of Yen coins. It then became apparent the placement of the devices was intended for an efficient payment process for your meal.

Smart Planning Tip #2. Japan is a very clean country, meaning you won't find refuse or rubbish bins in convenient locations. Often, during the middle of the day, if someone in our travel party needed a snack, whatever wrapper that snack came in would be placed in a backpack or a pocket until we entered the next train station. I highly recommend carrying empty plastic bags during the day as temporary trash bags until you get to a train station or a tourist attraction with a trash bin where you can empty your trash. Japan takes great pride in the cleanliness of their cities, and scattered litter while walking anywhere in the cities was almost non-existent.

Smart Planning Tip #3. Use technology to make your life easier! As a traveler in a foreign land, there is always a language barrier. The great thing about Japan is the Japanese people are VERY used to tourists meandering around their cities. Because of their acceptance of tourists, the language barrier is not nearly as bad as we expected. Many restaurants have picture menus for tourists to order from. Train station information and infographics displayed on trains accommodate English-speaking tourists. Some of the packaging found in convenience stores for quick snacks or meals is printed in Kanji and English to aid the purchaser. I recommend installing a good translator app on your smart device as it is sometimes handy. Additionally, a good maps app on your smart device is a must-have. Our travel party particularly liked Japan Travel by Navitime Japan Co. LTD. This app is free but offers a paid upgrade for long-term travelers in Japan. The app's free version saves multiple itineraries, with directions and routes to reach the attractions by train. The app includes an in-app map of train stations, ATMs, free Wi-Fi zones, and more. All in all, it was a worthy app to have at your fingertips, especially because you could enter a starting point and ending destination, and it would display the trains, routes, and train times that would get you to your destination.

Finally, the rental Wi-Fi options within Japan are very well worth the expense. Most train stations have free wifi, but when you're out walking through a beautiful park, temple, or shrine, it's nice to be still connected as very frequently someone needs to use data to check a train schedule or look for nearby restaurants. There are three or four WiFi rental agencies within Haneda airport that all offer the WiFi module, a spare battery pack, a plug and cord for charging, instructions to get connected, and a return envelope in which to drop your WiFi module in a Red post box station as you depart from Haneda airport. The cost of the stay-connected WiFi units was approximately $ 3.50 USD each day of use and provided connectivity at the speed advertised. Additionally, the ability to drop the unit into a clearly marked box as we walked into the airport for our departure flight couldn't have been any more convenient than it was. A tip I learned around the third day of our trip was a lightbulb moment for me. The WiFi rental companies all provide a spare battery pack as the WiFi modules are unlikely to last a full day. After the second day of wondering why the data module was seemingly nearly dead about halfway through the day, I realized that the included battery packs were intended to be connected to the WiFi module all day using the supplied short cord. A constant connection to the battery pack provides worry-free WiFi all day, and then you only need to charge the battery pack overnight instead of both the WiFi module and the battery pack.

Smart Planning Tip #4. Luggage. With the breadth of available luggage on the market today, it's hard to know which types and styles of luggage will be most conducive for good travel. A plain old suitcase with a hinge and handle would not be your friend if your travel plans were anything like ours, and that was to spend a few days in each of the cities we were visiting. Our itinerary required us to arrive at a rental location no less than four times and pack up a few days later to reach our next destination. There were numerous luggage styles within our travel party, with the most popular being the ever-present roller luggage with wheels that weren't designed for cobblestone-like terrain, which is often found in Japan. A few of us had traveler-style "backpacking" packs, which were rather large duffel-style bags that had thick padded shoulder straps and typically had a small "day pack" as a companion that doubles as a carry-on bag for flight and would be used as our day trip bags as well. Japan has many sets of stairs; it doesn't matter the region or prefecture, you're going to find stairs. The only escalators noted within Japan were at Haneda airport, and typically, there would be escalators in the larger Shinkansen stations on the outgoing (or exiting) side. Most subway train stations within the cities had flights of stairs on the station's entrance and exit sides, and traveling with wheeled roller bags was a constant exercise of lowering and extending the handle. The backpack-style duffel bags seemed the easiest to travel with, given the often ten-minute walks to a train station. With the flights of stairs at the train stations, it seemed easier to manage a pack on your back than a rolling piece of luggage that wasn't built for tiled floors or uneven ground, but we made it work. In our travel party, we had three people who used an Osprey brand travel pack, and these packs were built for exactly what we were doing, which was exploring Japan as urban Nomads. I highly recommend the Osprey brand; they are built for the journey and are rugged and durable.

DAY TRIPS

Wearing a day pack is highly recommended if you plan to be a "walking" nomadic tourist within the cities. The day packs (typically just a backpack) were handy as they carried whatever we needed during the day, such as light jackets, sunscreen, bottled water, and snacks. We also had our passports, which is a requirement for travelers in Japan as per the Japanese Government. We did need to show our passports at some of the attractions we visited, so keep that in mind. Typically, the night before the following day's trip, we would plan our day starting with train schedules and available convenience stores near our destination train stations. We would hone in on the weather for the day. Weather plays a key role in day trips when your dry feet are your best friend, and there was more than one instance where umbrellas would have come in handy.

Another tip for day tripping in Japan is to carry empty plastic bags for on-the-go trash receptacles. As stated, Japan is a very clean country, and there aren't regular refuse bins on street corners for public use. On multiple occasions, we had to visit a convenience store to buy something inexpensive, like a bottle of water to dispose of our temporary trash bag.

As long as you remember to pack light and smart – you'll do just fine in Japan. The weather can change instantly in Japan, and if it were not for a Don Quijote store placed near one of our private rentals, we likely would have gone without umbrellas during an unexpected rainstorm that turned out to be an entire day of rain.

CULTURAL CUSTOMS AND ETIQUETTE TIPS

Japan has a rich cultural heritage and a strong emphasis on etiquette and respect. Familiarize yourself with some cultural customs to ensure you navigate the country with sensitivity. Learn basic Japanese greetings and phrases; even a simple effort can greatly enhance interactions. Follow local customs like bowing when greeting or showing gratitude. Respect sacred places by following guidelines for entering temples and shrines, like removing your shoes. Familiarize yourself with proper manners for dining, such as using chopsticks and saying "Itadakimasu" before a meal. Understanding and respecting Japanese customs will contribute to a positive and immersive experience.

Japan's cultural customs and etiquette play a significant role in daily life, reflecting the country's respect, harmony, and mindfulness values. By familiarizing yourself with these customs, you can show appreciation for Japanese culture and create positive interactions with locals. Here are some essential customs and etiquette tips to enhance your travel experience in Japan.

Basic Japanese greetings and phrases. Learning basic Japanese greetings and phrases can go a long way in establishing a connection with locals and showing respect. Standard greetings include "Konnichiwa" (hello), "Arigatou gozaimasu" (thank you), and "Sumimasen" (excuse me). Making an effort to communicate in Japanese, even if it's just simple phrases, demonstrates your interest in the local culture and can elicit warm responses from the people you encounter.

Bow when greeting or showing gratitude. Bowing is an integral part of Japanese culture and is used for various occasions, including greetings, expressing gratitude, and showing respect. A slight bow of the head or a more profound bow can be appropriate when meeting someone, depending on the situation. Return a bow when someone bows to you, and remember that a more profound bow is usually reserved for formal or solemn occasions.

Respect sacred places. Japan is home to numerous temples, shrines, and other holy sites with great cultural and religious significance. When visiting these places, respecting the customs and guidelines is essential. Remove your shoes and hats before entering temple buildings or traditional guesthouses. Maintain a quiet and respectful demeanor, refraining from loud conversations or disruptive behavior. Follow any instructions or restrictions, such as refraining from photography in certain areas or not touching artifacts.

Familiarize yourself with proper dining manners. An emphasis on respect, cleanliness, and consideration for others characterizes Japanese dining etiquette. When dining, it is customary to say "Itadakimasu" before starting a meal, which expresses gratitude for the food. Use chopsticks correctly, avoiding crossing them or sticking them vertically into the rice, as these actions are associated with funeral rituals. Slurping noodles, particularly ramen, is acceptable and indicates that you enjoy the dish.

Observe public behavior. Japanese society values politeness and consideration for others, even in public spaces. Avoid speaking loudly on public transportation, such as trains or buses, and switch your phone to silent mode. Dispose of trash responsibly by using designated bins or carrying it until you find one. When queuing, maintain a proper distance and avoid pushing or cutting in line. These small acts of courtesy contribute to a harmonious and respectful environment.

By familiarizing yourself with Japanese cultural customs and etiquette, you can navigate Japan with sensitivity, respect, and appreciation. Learning basic greetings and phrases, bowing when appropriate, respecting sacred places, observing proper dining manners, and exhibiting polite behavior in public spaces will help create meaningful connections with locals and enrich your overall travel experience. Remember, embracing these customs enhances your journey and shows admiration for Japan's rich cultural heritage.

Planning your trip to Japan requires careful consideration of visa requirements, itinerary planning, budgeting, and cultural customs. Conducting thorough research, preparing necessary documents, and creating a well-structured itinerary will ensure a smooth and rewarding journey. Understanding the optimal times to visit Japan and the associated considerations for each season will enhance your travel experience. By budgeting wisely and embracing cultural customs and etiquette, you'll be able to confidently navigate Japan and immerse yourself in its captivating beauty and rich heritage.

In the next chapter, you'll read how we arrived at our itinerary, the main cities we wanted to visit, and the must-see attractions within those cities. Before finalizing our itinerary, we narrowed down a list of approximately fifty attractions our travel group had all submitted as possibilities. We arrived at our final itinerary by researching the destinations of the Japan Rail Shinkansen trains, the walking time between train stations and subway stations, and the proximity of those attractions to restaurants and certain districts within those cities.

2

FIVE AMAZING CITIES

An action plan for your travel itinerary when visiting Japan is highly recommended. With the understanding that you'll want to visit as many cities as time allows, it's best to plan your cities and the attractions you want to see before ever touching down at the Haneda Japan International Airport. Each city that we talk about in this book is bustling with tourist attractions, shopping districts, great food, a rich history dating back hundreds of years, and more. You'll want to be sure to take in as much as possible, and that's why a plan of action is highly recommended.

Throughout history, the cities of Tokyo, Kyoto, Osaka, Hiroshima, and Kamakura in Japan managed to survive the reign of emperors, shoguns, and periods of civil unrest through resilience, adaptation, and cultural significance. Tokyo, as the capital city since the Meiji Restoration, experienced various political changes. It withstood the transition from the feudal era to a modern metropolis, adapting to the demands of industrialization and emerging as a center of political, economic, and technological progress. Kyoto, renowned for its historical and cultural significance, was the imperial capital for over millennia. Despite political shifts and power struggles, it retained its status as the cultural heart of Japan, preserving traditional arts, architecture, and customs. Osaka, a central economic hub and commercial center, navigated the changing tides of power by embracing trade and commerce. Its vibrant merchant culture and entrepreneurial spirit allowed it to thrive, adapting to different political climates and contributing to Japan's economic growth. Hiroshima faced the devastating impact of the atomic bombing in 1945 during World War II. Despite the destruction, the city rebuilt itself as a symbol of peace and resilience. It became a testament to the endurance of its people, fostering a spirit of reconciliation and serving as a reminder of the horrors of war. An ancient city with historical significance, Kamakura was the seat of Japanese power during the Kamakura period (1185-1333). While it faced civil unrest and political upheaval during that time, it preserved its cultural heritage and continued to attract visitors with its numerous temples, shrines, and natural beauty.

During our stay in Japan, we knew well ahead of time the cities that were a "must-see" and the towns that we might visit if time allowed or if we needed a "filler" day due to weather or other unforeseen factors that may have ruined our daily itinerary. We will give you an overview of each city we explored during our stay. The cities were randomly picked based on JR Rail's accessibility and certain tourist attractions we wanted to see. Collectively, these cities showcased the ability of Japanese society to adapt and endure. They demonstrated resilience in the face of changing political structures and civil unrest while preserving their unique cultural identities and historical treasures and contributing to Japan's overall development and prosperity.

The five cities we visited over eleven days were:

- **Tokyo**
- **Kyoto**
- **Osaka**
- **Hiroshima**
- **Kamakura**

Each of these five cities is rich in history, and each has a different story of Japan dating back through the centuries of Emporers, Shoguns, and civil unrest. The history of these cities dates back beyond seven centuries of imperial power over Japan, and each of these cities is proud of its ability to have withstood the changes throughout the years.

TOKYO

Tokyo is a dynamic and bustling metropolis where traditional charm seamlessly blends with modern marvels. Whether a solo traveler or a family on a budget, Tokyo offers many experiences that captivate you. This city has everything from iconic landmarks to vibrant neighborhoods, shopping delights, and cultural treasures. Let's delve into the heart of Tokyo and discover the best attractions and experiences for budget-conscious adventurers.

Tokyo is a city that never sleeps, pulsating with energy and excitement. Experience the vibrant atmosphere of Shinjuku, the neon-lit heart of Tokyo, where towering skyscrapers contrast with traditional izakayas (Japanese pubs). Lose yourself in the bustling streets of Akihabara, the electric town renowned for its anime and gaming culture. Marvel at the architectural brilliance of the Tokyo Skytree, offering panoramic views of the cityscape. Tokyo's blend of traditional and modern attractions creates an enchanting tapestry for budget travelers to explore.

There are many opportunities to immerse yourself in Tokyo's rich cultural heritage by visiting iconic landmarks that showcase the city's history and traditions. Explore the grandeur of the Imperial Palace, the official residence of the Emperor of Japan, and stroll through the serene gardens surrounding it. Discover the beauty of Meiji Shrine, a tranquil oasis nestled within the bustling city, where you can witness traditional Shinto rituals and pay respects at the sacred shrine.

Indulge in the vibrant neighborhoods that offer diverse experiences for every traveler. Wander through the historic district of Asakusa, where you can explore the majestic Senso-ji Temple and sample local street food in Nakamise Shopping Street. In contrast, dive into the trendy world of Harajuku, known for its eccentric fashion, quirky shops, and vibrant street art.

For shopping enthusiasts, Tokyo is a paradise. Unleash your inner shopaholic in districts like Ginza, Omotesando, and Shibuya, where you'll find many department stores, fashion boutiques, and trendy shops. Experience the excitement of Shibuya Crossing, one of the busiest intersections in the world, as a sea of people navigates the bustling streets.

Indulge your taste buds with a magical foodie adventure in Tokyo. The city offers a diverse culinary scene, from budget-friendly street food stalls to Michelin-starred restaurants. Savor traditional sushi at Tsukiji Fish Market or sample a bowl of steaming ramen at a local noodle shop. Take advantage of the opportunity to try authentic Japanese izakaya, where you can enjoy small plates of delicious food paired with various drinks.

Tokyo's efficient public transportation system makes exploring the city on a budget easy. Utilize the extensive subway network, including the iconic Yamanote Line, to navigate between neighborhoods and attractions. Consider purchasing a Suica or Pasmo card, allowing convenient and cashless travel on trains, buses, and even vending machines. In a later chapter, we will dive deeper into the highly convenient Suica card options.

In Tokyo, there is always something for everyone, from free cultural events and festivals to art exhibitions and live performances. Take advantage of the city's many free attractions, such as strolling through the trendy neighborhoods of Shimokitazawa or exploring tranquil parks like Ueno Park and Yoyogi Park.

Tokyo's charm lies in its ability to seamlessly blend tradition and modernity, offering travelers a captivating experience combining ancient temples' serenity and futuristic technology. Embrace the dynamic energy of this metropolis, immerse yourself in its rich culture, and create lasting memories as you explore the vibrant streets of Tokyo.

You can embrace the iconic landmarks that define Tokyo's image. Ascend the Tokyo Tower, an iconic city symbol, for breathtaking views of Tokyo's skyline. Immerse yourself in the frenzy of Shibuya Crossing, the world's busiest pedestrian intersection, as you navigate the crowds of people. Take advantage of the Imperial Palace, surrounded by beautiful gardens and historic walls, offering a glimpse into Japan's regal history. These landmarks provide a sense of awe and wonder and are accessible to all, even those on a budget.

Tokyo's neighborhoods are a treasure trove of unique experiences. Start your journey in Asakusa, where you can visit the majestic Senso-ji Temple, wander through Nakamise Shopping Street for traditional souvenirs, and savor delicious street food. Make your way to Ueno Park, where you can explore world-class museums and enjoy the picturesque Shinobazu Pond. For a taste of Tokyo's vibrant youth culture, head to Harajuku, renowned for its quirky fashion boutiques, street art, and iconic Takeshita Street. These neighborhoods showcase Tokyo's diversity and offer budget-friendly attractions for everyone.

Tokyo is a paradise for shoppers and food enthusiasts, even for budget-conscious shoppers. Stroll through Ameya-Yokocho Market, a bustling street where you can find everything from vintage clothing to electronics at affordable prices. Explore the vast array of culinary delights in the bustling food alleys of Shinjuku's Omoide Yokocho or the Tsukiji Fish Market, where you can savor fresh seafood and authentic Japanese cuisine.

Take advantage of the entertainment options, too. Catch a free traditional performance at the Tokyo Metropolitan Government Building or take in the complimentary, nearly full panoramic view of Tokyo from 660 feet (202 meters) above the Tokyo city streets from the Government Building observation decks. Tokyo offers a world of affordable experiences for every taste, whether museums, performances, food, skyline photo opportunities, or the rich history of the Japanese empires throughout the centuries.

Tokyo's cultural heritage is a treasure trove that beckons budget travelers to explore its traditional temples, enchanting gardens, and captivating museums. Amidst the dynamic and bustling metropolis, the city cherishes its roots and offers a glimpse into Japan's rich history. Find solace at Meiji Shrine, a sanctuary of tranquility amidst the bustling streets, where you can witness traditional Shinto rituals and admire the grandeur of the shrine. Step into the Hama-rikyu Gardens, a haven of serenity with meticulously landscaped gardens, teahouses, and picturesque ponds. These gardens offer a peaceful retreat from the urban hustle and a chance to experience the beauty of nature.

Tokyo's museums are a treasure trove of cultural artifacts and artistic masterpieces. Take advantage of free or discounted entry on certain days to experience Japan's history and art. The Tokyo National Museum boasts a vast collection of Japanese art, including samurai armor, delicate ceramics, and exquisite paintings. The Edo-Tokyo Museum offers a fascinating journey through the city's past, showcasing the vibrant Edo period and its transformation into modern-day Tokyo. Immerse yourself in the exhibits and better understand Japan's cultural heritage.

In addition to temples, gardens, and museums, Tokyo's neighborhoods are steeped in history. Stroll through the nostalgic streets of Yanaka, where traditional wooden houses, charming alleyways, and local shops exude old-world charm. Explore the historic district of Asakusa, home to the iconic Senso-ji Temple, where you can immerse yourself in the atmosphere of ancient Japan. These neighborhoods offer a glimpse into Tokyo's past and provide a unique cultural experience.

Tokyo's rich cultural heritage is not limited to grand monuments and museums. It permeates everyday life, from traditional tea ceremonies and sumo wrestling to seasonal festivals and local customs. Engage with the locals, participate in cultural activities, and embrace the traditions that have shaped Tokyo's identity.

As a budget traveler, you can fully immerse yourself in Tokyo's cultural heritage without straining your wallet. Take advantage of free or discounted entry options, explore lesser-known neighborhoods, and embrace the opportunity to connect with Japan's rich traditions. Tokyo is a city that cherishes its cultural heritage and invites you to be a part of its captivating story.

Tokyo is a city of endless possibilities, where the past and present intertwine harmoniously. Its vibrant neighborhoods, iconic landmarks, world-class shopping, and rich cultural heritage make it an ideal destination for budget-conscious travelers. From the allure of tradition to the excitement of modernity, Tokyo offers an unforgettable experience that won't strain your wallet. So pack your bags, embrace the adventure, and let Tokyo's charm captivate you on a budget-friendly journey you'll cherish forever.

KYOTO

Kyoto is considered the cultural heart of Japan, where the ancient and the contemporary coexist in perfect harmony. Renowned for its well-preserved traditional architecture, UNESCO World Heritage sites, and serene gardens, Kyoto offers a captivating journey into Japan's rich cultural heritage. Immerse yourself in the enchanting atmosphere of this city while staying within your budget. Let's explore the highlights of Kyoto and discover the best experiences for travelers seeking tranquility and tradition.

The streets and neighborhoods within Kyoto are living museums of Japan's rich cultural past. Wander through the enchanting district of Higashiyama, where you'll find narrow lanes lined with traditional wooden machiya houses, charming tea houses, and shops selling traditional crafts. Marvel at the architectural splendor of Nijo Castle, completed in 1626, and now a UNESCO World Heritage site known for its "nightingale floors" that chirp like birds in a serene forest. Kyoto's dedication to preserving its empirical and cultural heritage is a testament to its timeless beauty.

Kyoto also boasts a remarkable collection of UNESCO World Heritage sites, each offering a glimpse into Japan's storied history. Visit Kiyomizu-dera, a magnificent wooden temple perched on a hillside, offering breathtaking panoramic city views. Explore the vibrant vermillion gates of Fushimi Inari Shrine, a sacred site dedicated to the Shinto god of rice and agriculture, and don't miss the Golden Pavilion (Kinkaku-ji), a stunning Zen Buddhist temple covered in gold leaf, reflecting its beauty onto a tranquil pond. These iconic landmarks are accessible to all, allowing budget travelers to immerse themselves in Kyoto's cultural treasures.

Strolling through Kyoto, you'll soon realize Kyoto is a sanctuary of tranquility, blessed with exquisite gardens and Zen temples inviting contemplation and inner peace. Explore the otherworldly beauty of the Ryoan-ji Temple's rock garden, an oasis of harmony and simplicity. Experience the serenity of the Arashiyama Bamboo Grove, where towering bamboo stalks create a mesmerizing atmosphere. Enjoy a traditional tea ceremony in Kyoto's atmospheric tea houses, where you can savor matcha tea while admiring meticulously manicured gardens. These experiences offer a refuge from the city's hustle and bustle while fitting into a budget-friendly itinerary.

Step into traditional Japanese arts and culture by visiting Gion, Kyoto's most famous geisha district. Stroll along Hanami-koji Street, adorned with traditional machiya houses, teahouses, and exclusive shops. Keep an eye out for geisha and maiko (apprentice geisha) gracefully making their way to engagements. Experience the elegance of a traditional tea house performance or attend a traditional Japanese music concert. Gion offers an authentic glimpse into Kyoto's captivating past and provides budget travelers with a cultural experience.

Timing your visit to Kyoto during the cherry blossom season or autumn foliage is a breathtaking experience. Witness the city come alive in a sea of pink sakura blossoms during spring or embrace the vivid hues of red, orange, and gold that paint the city's landscapes during autumn. Explore the Philosopher's Path, a scenic canal lined with cherry trees, or visit Arashiyama's bamboo grove for a magical encounter with nature's beauty. These natural spectacles are open to all and offer unforgettable awe and wonder.

Kyoto, with its well-preserved architecture, UNESCO World Heritage sites, serene gardens, traditional arts, and seasonal beauty, is a city that invites you to step into a bygone era while staying within your budget. Immerse yourself in the cultural heart of Japan, where tradition and tranquility reign supreme. Let Kyoto's timeless charm guide you on a budget-friendly journey that will leave an indelible imprint on your heart and mind.

OSAKA

Osaka, regularly referenced as a vibrant and flavorful city, is known as the "Nation's Kitchen." With its lively atmosphere, bustling streets, and renowned food culture, Osaka offers an exhilarating experience for budget-conscious travelers. From iconic landmarks to delectable street food, Osaka is a treasure trove to explore. You can dive into the urban charms of this modern city and discover the best experiences for those seeking culinary delights and vibrant urban adventures without breaking the bank.

Osaka's nickname, the "Nation's Kitchen," speaks volumes about its culinary prowess. Treat your taste buds in the city's vibrant food culture by exploring the countless street food stalls known as yatai, offering mouthwatering delicacies. Sample the iconic takoyaki, octopus balls topped with savory sauce and bonito flakes, or try the delicious pancake-like okonomiyaki made with various ingredients. Don't forget to visit the vibrant Kuromon

Ichiba Market, where you can savor fresh seafood, local produce, and other culinary delights. Osaka is surely a paradise for food lovers on a budget.

Undoubtedly, Osaka has a lively atmosphere that seamlessly blends modernity with tradition. Travelers can immerse themselves in the vibrant energy of the Dotonbori district, known for its iconic neon signs, bustling shopping streets, and a wide array of restaurants. Explore the trendy Amerikamura (American Village) for its quirky fashion boutiques, vintage stores, and hip cafes. As night falls, you shouldn't think twice about experiencing Osaka's vibrant nightlife by exploring the bars and izakayas in the bustling districts of Namba and Umeda. Enjoying the urban charms of Osaka without straining your budget is very easily accomplished, as Osaka has something for everyone.

Osaka offers a range of must-visit attractions that cater to different interests. You can begin your exploration with Osaka Castle, a majestic symbol of the city's history, while wandering through its beautiful grounds and soaking in the historical ambiance. You can then head to the iconic Dotonbori district to capture the essence of Osaka's vibrant street life, indulge in local street food, and pose for a photo with the famous Glico Running Man sign. If you're a fan of theme parks, don't miss Universal Studios Japan, where thrilling rides, a bit of theme park attraction, and immersive experiences await. These attractions provide budget-friendly entertainment options for travelers of all ages.

Osaka's street food scene is legendary, making it a paradise for travelers with discerning palates. Join the locals in their love for takoyaki, delicious octopus-filled balls cooked to perfection on hot griddles. Explore the vibrant street food stalls in the Namba area or the nostalgic Shinsekai district, where you can savor local specialties at affordable prices. Make sure to try Osaka's version of okonomiyaki, a savory pancake topped with various ingredients grilled to perfection right before your eyes. Osaka's street food offers a mouthwatering journey into the city's culinary heritage.

Osaka's strategic location makes it an ideal gateway to other captivating destinations in the Kansai region. Take a day trip to Nara, known for its friendly deer and historic temples, including the famous Todai-ji Temple with its Great Buddha. Explore the vibrant city of Kobe, renowned for its Kobe beef and scenic waterfront. These neighboring cities offer unique experiences that can easily be incorporated into your budget-friendly itinerary, allowing you to uncover more of the Kansai region's wonders.

Osaka, the "Nation's Kitchen," beckons travelers with its vibrant food culture, urban charms, and accessible attractions. From savoring delectable street food to exploring bustling shopping streets and immersing yourself in the city's vibrant nightlife, Osaka offers an unforgettable experience for those on a budget. Let your taste buds guide you through the culinary delights while the city's lively atmosphere and iconic landmarks enchant you. Osaka is a city where vibrant urban adventures and budget-friendly explorations intertwine, leaving you with cherished memories.

HIROSHIMA

Though marked by its tragic history, Hiroshima has emerged as a symbol of peace and resilience. The city stands as a testament to the strength and determination of its people to rebuild and create a brighter future. A visit to Hiroshima is an opportunity to pay tribute to the victims of the atomic bombing and to gain a deeper understanding of the devastating impact of war.

The Hiroshima Peace Memorial Park is massive, and serves as a poignant reminder of the events that unfolded on that fateful day. It is a powerful symbol of Hiroshima's commitment to peace and its worldwide message of peace. Take a moment to reflect at the Peace Memorial Museum, where exhibits and artifacts tell the stories of the survivors and provide insights into the long-lasting effects of nuclear warfare. The park's iconic Peace Memorial Dome, a UNESCO World Heritage site, stands as a stark reminder of the destruction caused by the atomic bomb and symbolizes the city's commitment to peace. Stroll through the serene park adorned with memorials, statues, and the iconic Peace Flame. Visit the Peace Memorial Museum, which offers a comprehensive and moving account of the atomic bombing and its aftermath, and gain a deeper understanding of the human cost of war and the importance of fostering a peaceful future. These experiences, accessible to all, contribute to a profound journey of reflection and peace education. This was an absolute highlight of our trip, as unfortunate as that fateful day was. The people of Hiroshima are so welcoming to tourists from the West that it's hard to imagine that nearly everyone in Hiroshima is a descendant of the tens of thousands of Japanese who lost their lives that day. The People of Hiroshima welcome American tourists with open arms, as all they want to do is promote Peace so a tragedy like that never happens again.

Beyond its tragic history, Hiroshima offers much more to travelers. Explore the city's vibrant streets and witness its remarkable transformation into a modern, thriving metropolis. Indulge in Hiroshima's culinary delights, including the famous Hiroshima-style okonomiyaki, a savory pancake layered with noodles, vegetables, and meat or seafood. Sample local delicacies at the bustling food markets and enjoy the warm hospitality of the locals.

Nature enthusiasts will find solace in Hiroshima's beautiful surroundings. Take a ferry to the serene Miyajima Island, known for its iconic floating torii gate and ancient Itsukushima Shrine. Immerse yourself in the island's tranquil atmosphere and enjoy scenic hikes through lush forests and picturesque landscapes. The breathtaking views of the Seto Inland Sea and the surrounding mountains will leave a lasting impression.

Hiroshima's resilience and commitment to peace extend beyond its borders. The city actively promotes peace education and international cooperation through various initiatives. Visitors can engage in cultural exchange programs, attend lectures on peace-related topics, and participate in workshops encouraging dialogue and understanding.

A visit to Hiroshima is a powerful and humbling experience as it serves as a reminder of the importance of peace, resilience, and the strength of the human spirit. By exploring Hiroshima, you pay tribute to its past and become part of the city's mission to create a more peaceful and harmonious world.

Travelers to Hiroshima can also immerse themselves in Hiroshima's rich cultural heritage by visiting its iconic attractions. Explore Hiroshima Castle, a reconstructed fortress that showcases traditional Japanese architecture and offers panoramic views of the city. Wander through the picturesque Shukkeien Garden, a tranquil oasis featuring meticulously landscaped gardens, tea houses, and serene ponds. Don't miss a trip to Miyajima Island, home to the iconic Itsukushima Shrine with its breathtaking floating torii gate. These attractions provide a glimpse into Japan's storied past and offer budget-friendly experiences for travelers.

Hiroshima embraces modernity while preserving its historical legacy. Experience the city's vibrant cityscape, bustling streets, modern architecture, and lively atmosphere. Explore the bustling shopping arcades, where you can find local specialties, souvenirs, and affordable dining options. Hiroshima's local cuisine, including Hiroshima-style okonomiyaki, offers a delectable culinary experience without straining your budget. Engage with the warm and welcoming locals, who will happily share their stories and recommendations, creating a truly immersive and budget-friendly experience.

Hiroshima's allure extends beyond its tragic history. Discover the city's natural beauty by exploring the scenic Hiroshima Bay, relaxing in its peaceful parks, or taking a tranquil cruise along the Ota River. Immerse yourself in its vibrant cultural scene by attending traditional performances, such as Noh theater or taiko drumming. Hiroshima also serves as a gateway to the nearby enchanting island of Okunoshima, famous for its population of friendly rabbits. These diverse experiences make Hiroshima a city of immense depth and offer budget-friendly opportunities for exploration.

As you stroll through this city, there's no doubt that Hiroshima invites you on a journey of hope, resilience, and peace. From its poignant reminders of history to its vibrant cityscape, cultural attractions, and welcoming locals, the city offers a blend of experiences that can be enjoyed on a budget. Embrace Hiroshima's rich cultural heritage, explore its natural beauty, and engage with the spirit of resilience that permeates the city. As you depart, carry with you the lessons of peace and harmony that Hiroshima so passionately imparts.

KAMAKURA

Walking into Kamakura, you immediately realize that this coastal town encapsulates historical significance, picturesque beauty, and a tranquil atmosphere. Kamakura offers a captivating journey into Japan's rich cultural heritage, from the iconic Great Buddha to the array of temples and shrines. Surrounded by breathtaking coastal scenery and lush nature, the town beckons budget-conscious travelers to explore its hidden gems and indulge in outdoor activities.

Kamakura's coastal setting adds a touch of enchantment to its historical allure. Immerse yourself in the town's unique atmosphere as you stroll its charming streets and catch glimpses of the shimmering sea. Kamakura has a tourist-friendly feel, and many locally owned surf and gift shops are Hawaiian expatriots from the USA who have relocated to Kamakura and set up businesses to serve the constant passage of tourists throughout the city. Kamakura's historical significance as the former political center of medieval Japan is palpable, with remnants of its glorious past still evident in its architecture and cultural landmarks.

A visit to Kamakura would be incomplete without marveling at the iconic Great Buddha (Daibutsu) at the Kōtoku-in temple. This magnificent bronze statue stands at an impressive height, creating a sense of awe and reverence. Admire the intricate details of the statue and contemplate its historical significance as you explore the serene surroundings of Kotokuin Temple. The Great Buddha is a must-see highlight that captures the essence of Kamakura's historical grandeur.

Discovering Kamakura's spiritual side by visiting its renowned temples and shrines is a must for travelers visiting this quaint seaside town. Hasedera Temple, perched on a hillside, offers panoramic views of the town and houses a collection of exquisite Buddhist art. Tsurugaoka Hachimangu Shrine, with its majestic wooden gate and vibrant atmosphere, invites visitors to immerse themselves in traditional Japanese culture and rituals. These sacred sites provide an immersive experience of Kamakura's religious heritage.

Kamakura's coastal location offers a haven for relaxation and natural beauty. Take a break from historical exploration and unwind at the town's beautiful beaches, such as Yuigahama Beach and Zaimokuza Beach. Soak up the sun, feel the gentle breeze, and listen to the soothing sound of the ocean waves. These serene beaches provide budget-friendly options for rejuvenation and a peaceful retreat amidst Kamakura's historical charm.

Kamakura's natural splendor extends beyond its coastal allure. Embrace the town's lush greenery and embark on hiking trails that meander through its picturesque surroundings. Visit Kamakura's bamboo groves or explore the trails leading to iconic spots like the Zeniarai Benten Shrine or the Zen temples of Kenchoji and Engakuji. These outdoor activities allow you to connect with nature, soak in the tranquil ambiance, and rejuvenate your senses while staying within your budget.

Kamakura, with its historical significance, coastal beauty, and opportunities for outdoor exploration, invites you on a journey of discovery and tranquility. Immerse yourself in the town's rich cultural heritage, marvel at the iconic Great Buddha, and find solace in the picturesque coastal scenery. Kamakura's fusion of history and nature creates a unique experience for budget-conscious travelers seeking serenity and immersion. Embrace the town's captivating charms, and let Kamakura weave its magic upon you.

One of the hidden gems of Kamakura that quite often does not make it to travel books is the Enoshima Sea Candle. Enoshima is a small offshore Island connecting to Kamakura from a bridge with a well-placed walking path. Enoshima Island boasts the Sea Candle as a popular tourist attraction, and its placement at the top of Enoshima Island earns this must-see attraction a top spot. With full panoramic views of Kamakura and Fujisawa, it is another wonderful observation tower that will delight those looking for another view of Mount Fuji.

Without a doubt, any city of sizeable nature you visit while traveling in Japan will provide multiple days worth of sights, sounds, and smells, but Kamakura has the bonus of providing a tourist-friendly coastal town feel that cannot be matched.

3

ARRIVING BY AIR

WELCOME TO TOKYO!

UPON ARRIVAL AT HANEDA AIRPORT, you will proceed through the arrival procedures. Haneda Airport, officially known as Tokyo International Airport, is one of Japan's busiest and most important airports. It is located conveniently within Tokyo and is a major domestic and international travel gateway. Navigating Haneda Airport efficiently is crucial to starting your trip smoothly, including customs and immigration. Follow the signs to the immigration counters, where you will present your passport and any required documents for inspection. After clearing immigration, collect your luggage from the designated carousel and proceed to the customs area. Here, your bags may be subject to inspection, so ensure you are aware of any prohibited items to avoid any delays.

Once you have cleared customs, it's time to consider your ground transportation options to Tokyo. Haneda Airport offers various transportation methods, including trains, buses, taxis, and private transfers. The most popular and convenient option is the train. Haneda Airport has a train station providing direct connections to various parts of Tokyo. The Keikyu Line and Tokyo Monorail are two major train lines that serve the airport and offer quick and efficient transportation to popular destinations in the city.

Being familiar with its layout and facilities helps navigate the airport efficiently. Haneda Airport has three terminals: Terminal 1, Terminal 2, and the International Terminal. Each terminal has its check-in counters, security checkpoints, and departure gates. Please check your airline and terminal information to ensure a smooth departure process. The airport provides clear signage in both Japanese and English, making it easy to navigate between different areas.

It's also important to plan your time wisely when navigating Haneda Airport. Allow ample time for check-in, security procedures, and immigration clearance, especially during peak travel. Additionally, take advantage of the airport's amenities, such as duty-free shops, restaurants, and lounges, to make your waiting time more enjoyable.

In summary, Haneda Airport plays a crucial role in Japan's air transportation network, and navigating it efficiently is essential for a smooth travel experience. Familiarize yourself with arrival procedures, customs, and immigration processes, and consider your ground transportation options to Tokyo. With proper planning and awareness of the airport's layout, you can easily navigate Haneda Airport and start your journey in Japan on the right foot.

CUSTOMS AT HANEDA AIRPORT

First and foremost, every traveler to Japan must provide the required information, which can be found on the website titled

"Visit Japan Web." However, there is no direct link to the website through an internet search. If you enter "Visit Japan Web" into an internet browser, you will find an internet link that says Visit Japan Web | Digital Agency, and this is the link you should choose to be taken to the Visit Japan Web website. On the Visit Japan website, you can provide your passport information. Your customs declarations (as to what chemicals, medicines, etc., you are bringing into the country), and the best part is you won't be left at the customs counter filling out stacks of paperwork to comply with the Japanese regulations for foreign entry into their country.

Once completed with the Visit Japan Web information entry, you will be provided with a QR code you show the customs agents upon entry into the country, and you will breeze right through customs.

PURCHASING YOUR JR RAIL PASS

Purchasing your JR Rail Pass voucher before arriving at Haneda Airport is highly recommended to ensure a smooth and efficient travel experience. Buying your JR Rail Pass in advance allows you to skip the lines and exchange your voucher for the actual pass more quickly at the JR Rail offices in the airport. You can purchase a JR Rail voucher from various JR Rail voucher providers online; however, the most popular and the one that our travel party had an efficient and flawless process with was jrrailpass.com. Multiple providers sell exchange vouchers that can be later exchanged for the JR Pass at designated locations, including Haneda Airport. Reach the JR Rail office within the airport terminals upon arrival at Haneda Airport. Present your voucher and passport to the office staff, who will verify your information and exchange the voucher for the actual JR Pass. The staff will provide instructions, a guidebook, and assistance in making seat reservations if needed. By purchasing your JR Rail Pass in advance from any authorized JR Rail voucher provider, you can secure your pass, save time at Haneda Airport, and enjoy the benefits of unlimited travel on the JR network right away.

Some of the popular JR Rail voucher providers include:

- **Japan-Rail-Pass.com.** The official provider of the JR Pass offers a wide range of pass options for different durations and classes. You can purchase the JR Pass online through their official website and receive a voucher that can be exchanged for the pass upon arrival.
- **JRailPass.com.** An authorized agent for the JR Pass, offering convenient online purchase options. They provide e-tickets or physical vouchers that can be exchanged for the JR Pass at the airport.
- **Klook.** A well-known travel booking platform offering JR Rail Pass vouchers for purchase online. You can choose from various pass options and receive a voucher that can be exchanged for the JR Pass at Haneda Airport.

To buy a JR Rail voucher from any provider, visit their respective websites, select the desired pass type and duration, and proceed with the payment. You will receive a confirmation email containing the voucher or e-ticket, which, if you have a voucher (also called an exchange ticket), you must present it at the JR Rail office in Haneda Airport for exchange. Some of these providers of a JR Rail Voucher will mail your voucher within days of your purchase.

JR RAIL OFFICES

When navigating Haneda Airport, it's important to note that JR Rail offices are conveniently located within the airport, where you can exchange your JR Pass for the actual JR tickets. The JR Pass is a popular option for travelers exploring Japan using the extensive JR (Japan Railways) network.

After clearing customs and collecting your luggage, head towards the arrival area and look for the signs indicating the JR Rail offices. These offices are typically located near the train stations within the airport terminals. Haneda Airport has JR East Travel Service Centers catering to domestic and international travelers.

At the JR Rail office, you can present your JR Pass voucher, which you might have obtained before your trip or purchased at the airport, along with your passport. The staff will assist you in exchanging the voucher for the actual JR Pass, a valuable ticket granting unlimited access to JR trains for a specific time.

The JR Rail office staff will also provide a detailed guidebook or map outlining the coverage and services available with the JR Pass. They can assist you in planning your train journeys, make seat reservations for specific routes, and answer any questions about the JR network.

Once you have exchanged your JR Pass, you can go to the appropriate JR train station at Haneda Airport to board your desired train. The JR lines at the airport connect to various destinations within Tokyo and beyond, allowing you to travel to popular cities like Kyoto, Osaka, and Hiroshima conveniently.

Navigating Haneda Airport to find the JR Rail offices and exchange your JR Pass for the actual JR tickets ensures a smooth transition into utilizing the extensive JR network for your travel throughout Japan. It's recommended that you check the operating hours of the JR Rail offices in advance and allocate enough time for this process, especially during busy periods. Having your JR Pass ready allows you to make seat reservations and enjoy unlimited train travel hassle-free.

Please remember, when navigating Haneda Airport, you can go to the JR Rail offices within the airport terminals to exchange your JR voucher for the actual JR tickets. The friendly staff will help you in this process and guide you using the JR network during your journey in Japan. By taking advantage of the JR Pass and the convenience of the JR Rail offices, you can enjoy seamless travel and easily explore the country.

ARRIVAL, CUSTOMS, AND IMMIGRATION

Upon arriving at Haneda Airport, it is essential to know the arrival procedures, customs, and immigration processes to ensure a smooth entry into Japan. Here's a detailed overview:

> **Arrival Procedures.** After disembarking from the aircraft, follow the signs for Immigration and Baggage Claim. As you enter the terminal building, you will be guided to the immigration area. Ensure your passport, completed arrival card (received during the flight or available at the airport), and any necessary visa or entry permit are ready for inspection.

Smart Planning Tip #5: To save loads of time at that airport when going through customs and immigration, have your QR code handy if you've pre-filled your customs paperwork on the Visit Japan Website found here: https://vjw-lp.digital.go.jp/en/. This website is a digital version of all customs or immigration paperwork needed to enter Japan. Upon completing the paperwork, a QR code is issued to the registered user for customs and immigration you can provide for the agent. This is a definite time saver at the airport.

Immigration Process. At the immigration counters, present your passport, arrival card, and other required documents to the immigration officer unless you come ready with the QR codes you received after completing your registration on Visit Japan Web. They will verify your passport, check your visa or landing permit, and ask a few questions about the purpose and duration of your visit. Once cleared, the officer will stamp your passport, granting you entry into Japan.

Baggage Claim. After passing through immigration, proceed to the designated baggage claim area. Look for electronic display boards or screens that indicate the carousel number assigned to your flight. Retrieve your checked luggage and ensure that you have all your belongings.

Customs Declaration. Proceed to the customs declaration area after collecting your luggage. Japan has specific regulations regarding importing certain items, including restricted goods and duty-free allowances. If you have items that exceed the duty-free limits or fall under restricted categories, you must declare them. Follow the signs for either the "Goods to Declare" (red channel) or "Nothing to Declare" (green channel) based on your situation.

Customs Inspection. Customs inspections at Haneda Airport are usually random or based on suspicion. If you are directed to the red channel or selected for review, follow the instructions of the customs officer. They may ask you to inspect your luggage or inquire about the contents of what you are carrying. Be cooperative and answer any questions truthfully. If you have nothing to declare, proceed through the green channel without being stopped.

Quarantine Procedures. Haneda Airport has a separate area for quarantine inspections, which may be conducted for health and safety purposes. In the event of a quarantine inspection, follow the instructions given by the authorities and provide any necessary information or documentation. As of 2023, Japan no longer requires foreign travelers to be placed into quarantine.

It is important to note that Haneda Airport provides clear signage and instructions in multiple languages to guide passengers through the arrival procedures. The airport staff and officials are generally helpful and approachable, so feel free to seek assistance if needed by familiarizing yourself with these arrival procedures, customs, and immigration processes at Haneda Airport. You can easily ensure a smooth entry into Japan and start your journey.

GROUND TRANSPORTATION

Haneda Airport offers various convenient ground transportation options to reach Tokyo and its surrounding areas. Here are some of the popular options available:

Train. One of the most efficient and cost-effective ways to travel from Haneda Airport to Tokyo is by train. The Tokyo Monorail connects the airport to Hamamatsucho Station, from where you can transfer to other train lines to reach your desired destination. The journey to central Tokyo takes approximately 15-30 minutes, depending on the destination. Another train option is the Keikyu Line, which connects stations like Shinagawa and Yokohama.

Limousine Bus. Limousine buses are convenient for travelers with large luggage or those heading directly to specific hotels. These buses operate regular services between Haneda Airport and major hotels in Tokyo, offering a comfortable and direct transportation option. The bus stops are near the terminal exits, and you can purchase tickets at the counters or vending machines in the arrival lobby.

Taxi. Taxis and cabs are readily available at the taxi stands outside each terminal. While taxis can be more expensive compared to other options, they provide a door-to-door service and can be a good choice if you have a lot of luggage or prefer a more private and convenient mode of transportation. It's important to note that taxi fares in Japan are metered and can vary based on factors such as distance and time.

Shared Shuttles. Shared shuttle services, such as the Airport Limousine Bus or private shuttle companies, offer another transportation option from Haneda Airport to Tokyo. These services operate on fixed routes and schedules, picking up passengers from the airport and dropping them off at major hotels or designated locations in Tokyo. Shared shuttles can be convenient if you prefer a more affordable and organized transfer.

Rental Cars. If you prefer the freedom to explore at your own pace, you can rent a car from Haneda Airport. Several car rental companies have counters located in the arrival lobbies, and you can make a reservation in advance or directly at the airport. Before considering this option, it's essential to familiarize yourself with driving rules and regulations in Japan, including traffic rules and parking options.

When choosing a ground transportation option, consider your destination, budget, luggage, and personal preferences. Planning and researching the best option based on your needs is advisable to ensure a smooth and efficient journey from Haneda Airport to Tokyo.

NAVIGATING HANEDA AIRPORT

Navigating the airport efficiently is essential to save time and have a smooth travel experience at Haneda Airport. Here are some tips to help you navigate the airport efficiently:

Arrive Early. To avoid any last-minute rush or delays, arrive at the airport before your flight. You should plan to arrive at least two to three hours before your scheduled departure time, especially for international flights. This extra time allows you to complete check-in, security, and other necessary procedures without feeling rushed.

Check-in Online. You can take advantage of online check-in services offered by your airline. This allows you to check in and select your seats in advance, saving you time at the airport. Some airlines also offer mobile boarding passes, which can be stored on your smartphone for easy access.

Follow Signage. Haneda Airport has clear signage in both Japanese and English to guide passengers through various areas of the airport. Pay attention to the signs and follow the directions to reach your desired locations, such as check-in counters, security checkpoints, and departure gates. The signs also indicate the locations of facilities like restrooms, lounges, and dining areas.

Security Check. Be prepared for the security screening process by following the guidelines provided. Place your belongings in separate trays for X-ray screening, including carry-on bags, laptops, and liquids. Remember to remove any metal objects or electronics from your pockets and follow instructions from the security personnel. This will help ensure a quick and hassle-free security check experience.

Terminal Layout. Haneda Airport has multiple terminals, so please familiarize yourself with the layout before you arrive. Each terminal has its own facilities, including check-in counters, security checkpoints, and departure gates. Knowing the terminal you will depart from or arrive at will help you navigate the airport more efficiently and avoid confusion.

Airport Facilities. Haneda Airport offers many facilities and amenities to enhance your travel experience. These include duty-free shops, restaurants, currency exchange counters, luggage storage, and shower rooms. If you have a long layover or early arrival, use these facilities to relax, dine, or freshen up before continuing your journey. One of the most popular facilities travelers use at Haneda Airport is the plethora of restaurants throughout the terminal. On busy travel days, the restaurants get backed up just like any non-airport restaurant, as some restaurants take up to an hour from your order to food delivery.

Stay Connected. Haneda Airport provides free Wi-Fi throughout the terminals, allowing you to stay connected and access important information. Connect to the airport's Wi-Fi network and use airline or travel apps to receive real-time updates on flight status, gate changes, and other relevant information.

We've covered quite a bit in this chapter, and I hope you are already shedding some of your pre-trip planning anxiety. The plethora of information in this chapter is simply from the convenience of having the trip behind us and being able to retrospectively assess what we knew before arriving and what we learned on the fly while traversing Japan's borders.

From WiFi connectivity to restaurants and ground transportation to the convenience of having a QR code at hand while going through customs, arriving at the Haneda Tokyo International Airport is not unlike arriving at an international airport anywhere else in the world, except for one thing: the Tokyo airport is one of the largest in the Eastern world. The large volume of travelers in the airport can sometimes make navigating and keeping a schedule hard to follow, and there are natives and travelers everywhere in the airport.

Following these tips, you can navigate Haneda Airport efficiently, save time, and have a stress-free travel experience. You can familiarize yourself with the airport layout, be prepared for security checks, and use the available facilities. This way, you can focus on enjoying your journey while effectively maneuvering through the airport and venturing out into the fantastic city of Tokyo.

4

UNDERSTANDING THE RAIL SYSTEM

AN EFFECTIVE RAIL SYSTEM

JAPAN BOASTS one of the most efficient and reliable rail systems in the world, making it the preferred mode of transportation for many Japanese natives and travelers. The rail system in Japan has a rich history that dates back to the late 19th century. The first railway line, the Tōkaidō Main Line, was inaugurated in 1872 and connected Tokyo with Yokohama. This marked the beginning of Japan's modern rail network. Over the years, the rail system expanded rapidly, connecting major cities and regions throughout the country.

In addition to conventional railways, Japan is renowned for its efficient subway systems. Tokyo's subway system, for example, is one of the busiest and most extensive in the world, serving millions of passengers daily. Other major cities, such as Osaka and Kyoto, also have well-developed subway networks, offering convenient transportation within urban areas.

One of Japan's most iconic rail innovations is the Shinkansen, the bullet train. The first Shinkansen line, the Tōkaidō

Shinkansen, opened in 1964 in time for the Tokyo Olympics. This high-speed rail network revolutionized travel in Japan, allowing passengers to reach speeds of up to 200 mph (320 km/h). The Shinkansen quickly became synonymous with safety, punctuality, and comfort, attracting domestic and international travelers.

Since its introduction, the Shinkansen network has expanded to multiple lines, connecting major cities across Japan. Today, travelers can enjoy the convenience and speed of the Shinkansen when exploring nearly the entire country. With its sleek design and advanced technology, the bullet train remains a symbol of Japan's commitment to innovation and excellence in transportation.

Overall, Japan's rail system, encompassing conventional railways, subway networks, and the renowned Shinkansen, has played a crucial role in the country's economic development and has become an integral part of Japanese culture. Its efficiency, reliability, and extensive coverage make it an excellent choice for domestic and international travelers seeking to explore Japan's diverse regions and cities.

To make the most of your train travel experience in Japan, it's essential to understand the rail network, ticketing procedures, and how to navigate train stations.

OVERVIEW OF JAPAN'S EFFICIENT RAIL NETWORK

Japan's rail network is extensive, connecting major cities and regions with a comprehensive system of trains. The Shinkansen, or bullet train, is renowned for its speed and punctuality, allowing you to traverse long distances quickly. Regional and local trains cover shorter routes, providing access to smaller towns and attractions. The rail system is well-integrated, making it convenient to travel nationwide. In Japan, train stations are well-equipped to accommodate foreign travelers, with many signs and announcements displayed in both Japanese and English. While the level of English translation may vary depending on the station's size and location, understanding a few essential phrases can greatly assist travelers in navigating the train system.

When moving through train stations, you can expect to encounter signage that provides information in both Japanese and English. Station names, platform numbers, and directional signs are typically displayed in both languages, making it easier to find your way around. However, it's worth noting that smaller or rural stations may have limited English signage, so having a basic grasp of crucial phrases and symbols can be helpful.

Train announcements in major cities and popular tourist areas are commonly made in Japanese and English. These announcements typically include essential details such as the next station, transfer options, and any delays or schedule changes. By listening to these announcements, foreign travelers can stay informed and ensure they disembark at the correct station.

Most train stations provide ticket machines with an English-language option when purchasing tickets. This allows travelers to navigate the menu, select their destination, and choose the type of ticket they require. The interface generally offers options for one-way or round-trip tickets and calculates the fare accordingly. If you need help, station staff are often available to help with ticket purchases, directions, and other questions.

While communication with station staff may only sometimes be smooth due to language barriers, they are usually eager to assist travelers, and simple gestures of politeness can go a long way. Additionally, fellow travelers in Japan are often willing to lend a hand or share helpful information. Don't hesitate to politely contact other tourists if you need guidance or have questions about navigating the train system.

By being aware of the availability of English translations, familiarizing yourself with key phrases, and seeking assistance, you can safely navigate train stations in Japan and make the most of your travel experience.

Different types of rail passes and their benefits. Japan offers various rail passes that provide unlimited travel on designated lines for a fixed period. The most popular is the Japan Rail Pass (JR Pass), which allows unlimited travel on JR lines, including the Shinkansen. This pass is available for different durations and is a cost-effective option for travelers planning multiple long-distance journeys. Regional passes, such as the JR West Pass or JR East Pass, cater to specific areas and can be advantageous if you explore a particular region in depth.

You are navigating train stations, purchasing tickets, and using ticket machines. Japan train stations can be bustling hubs, but you can easily navigate them with a few tips. Please look for signs and overhead displays indicating platforms, train lines, and destinations. Self-service ticket machines are typically available near the entrance or on the platform. English language options are commonly available on these machines, making them convenient for international travelers. Select your destination, choose the type of ticket you need (e.g., one-way, round trip), and follow the prompts to purchase your ticket.

Planning and optimizing train travel between cities. When planning your train travel between cities, consider factors such as travel time, frequency of trains, and costs. Use online resources like Hyperdia or Google Maps to check train schedules, fares, and transfer information. Optimize your travel by choosing the most efficient routes, considering direct trains and connections. You'll need to book reserved seats for long-distance journeys on the Shinkansen (especially if you have luggage) during peak travel to ensure you're available. The Shinkansen trains most always have on-board restrooms, and the longer route trains typically offer snack service from a train attendant who can provide coffee, water, bento-style meal boxes, candy, and more.

Essential Japanese phrases for train travel. While many train station signs and announcements in Japan are displayed in both Japanese and English, knowing a few essential phrases can be helpful. Here are some key phrases to familiarize yourself with:

- "Eki wa doko desu ka?" (Where is the station?)

- "Kippu o kudasai" (One ticket, please.)

- "Tokyo eki made ikimasu" (I'm going to Tokyo Station.)

- "Noriba wa doko desu ka?" (Where is the platform?)

- "Eki o deru jikan wa nanji desu ka?" (What time does the train depart?)

- "Arigatou gozaimasu" (Thank you very much.)

THE CONVENIENCE OF THE SUICA CARD

The Suica card is a convenient and widely used physical card or contactless smart card for public transportation in Japan, including train stations, subways, buses, and even some taxis. It offers a seamless and efficient way for travelers to enter and exit train stations without purchasing individual tickets.

The Suica card operates on a rechargeable system, allowing users to load money onto the card and use it to pay for fares. It eliminates the hassle of buying tickets for every journey and provides a more convenient travel experience. The card can be easily topped up at ticket machines or designated recharge machines at train stations, making it a time-saving option for frequent travelers. To use the Suica card, touch it on the card reader at the ticket gate when entering and exiting train stations. The fare is automatically deducted from the card's balance based on the distance traveled. This contactless system reduces the need for physical ticket handling and speeds up the process, especially during peak travel times.

One of the significant advantages of the Suica card is its versatility. It is not limited to a specific region or transportation operator, making it valid across most of Japan's major cities and regions. You can use the same card in Tokyo, Osaka, Kyoto, and many other places that have integrated their transportation systems with the Suica network. Additionally, the Suica card can be used for more than just transportation. It can be purchased at selected stores, vending machines, and convenience stores. This feature makes it a convenient all-in-one payment solution, allowing travelers to easily make small transactions during their journey.

Obtaining a Suica card is simple and can be done at major train stations or designated locations. The card has a small issuance fee, which is refundable upon return. It is a cost-effective and practical option for travelers who plan to use public transportation extensively during their stay in Japan.

The digital Suica card used with a smart device mobile wallet application is available for most smartphones and enhances the functionality and convenience of the Suica card system in Japan. With the digital Suica card installed on your smartphone, you can easily enjoy added features and manage your Suica card. One of the key features of the digital Suica card is the ability to recharge it digitally and on the fly as it's connected to a bank or credit card of your choice. Instead of using ticket or recharge machines at train stations, you can conveniently add funds to your Suica card directly from your smartphone. This eliminates the need to carry cash or find a physical location to recharge your card, making it incredibly convenient for travelers.

The digital Suica card also provides real-time information on your card balance, including recent transactions and usage history. This allows you to keep track of your spending and monitor your card's remaining balance. This information is readily available on your smartphone, helps you plan your travel expenses, and ensures that you always have sufficient funds on your digital Suica card. Another helpful feature of the digital Suica card is the ability to link your Suica card with a mobile payment service, such as Apple Pay or Google Pay. This enables you to use your smartphone to pay for transportation fares or purchases at stores accepting Suica card payments. It adds more convenience and flexibility to your payment options, especially if you prefer to use your smartphone for contactless transactions.

To use the digital Suica card through your smartphone's mobile wallet, you must create an account and register your credit card. The app is available for download on iOS and Android platforms and is compatible with various smartphone models.

Overall, the Suica card app enhances the functionality and convenience of the Suica card system, allowing you to manage your card, recharge it digitally, and access real-time information on your smartphone. Utilizing this app can make your travel experience in Japan smooth and more efficient.

From a convenience standpoint, the digital Suica card offers a seamless and convenient method for entering and exiting train stations in Japan. Its rechargeable nature, wide acceptance, and additional payment capabilities at restaurants, vending machines, and even the ever-present 7-11 stores make it an excellent choice for travelers looking for a hassle-free and efficient way to navigate the country's transportation system.

Understanding Japan's rail system is crucial for efficient and convenient travel. Familiarize yourself with the rail network, consider the benefits of different rail passes, and learn how to navigate train stations and purchase tickets. Plan your train travel between cities, optimizing routes and considering travel times. Knowing essential Japanese phrases related to train travel will also enhance your experience and help you communicate effectively. With this knowledge, you'll be well-prepared to explore Japan's fascinating destinations using its efficient rail system.

In the next chapter, we will dive into the unmatched array of dining options available in the cities on our Japanese adventure. so let your taste buds start to water, and dream about the incredible food that awaits you while you're in Japan!

5

DINING JAPANESE STYLE

Japanese cuisine is renowned for its delicate flavors, meticulous preparation, and emphasis on fresh, seasonal ingredients. It reflects the country's rich cultural heritage and deep connection to nature. To fully appreciate Japanese cuisine, it's important to understand its key aspects and dining culture.

Traditional Japanese cuisine, known as *washoku*, is based on balance, harmony, and simplicity principles. It often features rice, fish, seafood, vegetables, tofu, and seaweed. These ingredients are prepared with minimal seasoning, allowing their natural flavors to shine. Seasonality is vital, with dishes varying yearly to highlight the freshest produce and seafood available.

A typical Japanese meal consists of multiple small dishes served together. The "shushoku" is the main dish and is complemented by side dishes known as "okazu" and accompanied by rice and miso soup. This dining style allows a diverse range of flavors and textures to be enjoyed in a single meal.

In Japan, dining is not just about the food but also the overall experience. Restaurants in Japan often pay great attention to creating an inviting ambiance, whether it's a serene traditional setting or a modern and trendy atmosphere. Respectful and attentive service is also a hallmark of Japanese dining culture.

When dining out in Japan, showing gratitude and appreciation to the chef and staff is customary. At the beginning of the meal, it is common to say "Itadakimasu," which expresses gratitude for the food. At the end of the meal, saying "Gochisousama deshita" conveys appreciation for the delicious meal and the effort put into its preparation.

Japanese cuisine is not limited to high-end restaurants. The country offers various dining options to suit all budgets and preferences. There is something for everyone, from humble street food stalls to casual izakayas, traditional ryokans to Michelin-starred establishments.

Exploring different types of Japanese cuisine is a must when visiting Japan. Each culinary style has unique characteristics and flavors, from sushi and sashimi to ramen, tempura, yakitori, and kaiseki. Be open to trying new dishes and flavors, and don't hesitate to ask for recommendations or guidance from locals to discover hidden culinary gems.

Whether you indulge in a lavish multi-course kaiseki meal or enjoy a bowl of piping hot ramen at a humble noodle shop, experiencing Japanese cuisine is essential to any visit to Japan. It is an opportunity to savor the artistry and dedication that goes into each dish and to connect with the country's rich culinary heritage.

CULINARY DELIGHTS

Finding and choosing restaurants in Japan can be an exciting culinary adventure. Here are some valuable tips to help you navigate the vast culinary landscape and maximize your dining experiences.

Before your trip, take some time to research the local cuisine and popular dining areas in the cities you plan to visit. Look for recommendations from travel guides, online platforms, and fellow travelers. Creating a list of potential restaurants will give you a starting point and help you make informed decisions.

Each neighborhood in Japan has its own unique food scene. Venture beyond the tourist hotspots and explore local neighborhoods to discover hidden gems. These areas often offer authentic and affordable dining options that locals favor.

Expert Tip: One of the best indicators of a good restaurant is a crowded dining establishment with locals. If you see a restaurant full of Japanese customers or a long line of Japanese natives waiting outside, it's a good sign that the food is delicious and authentic. Don't be afraid to follow the locals' lead and try out their favorite spots.

Many restaurants in Japan display realistic food replicas, known as "sampuru," in their windows or at the entrance. These replicas visually represent the dishes they serve and can be helpful when deciding where to eat, especially if you don't speak Japanese. Look for restaurants with appealing displays that catch your eye.

In some small local eateries, particularly ramen shops, you may encounter ticket vending machines instead of ordering directly from the staff. These machines allow you to select and pay for your meal in advance by inserting yen and pressing the corresponding buttons for your desired dishes. Once you receive your tickets, hand them to the staff, and they will prepare your order. Don't be intimidated by these machines—they are straightforward and can lead you to fantastic dining experiences.

Participate in food-focused activities such as food tours, cooking classes, or market visits. These experiences can introduce you to local ingredients, culinary traditions, and unique dining spots. You'll gain insights into Japanese cuisine while enjoying the opportunity to taste various dishes.

Don't hesitate to seek recommendations from locals, hotel staff, or fellow travelers. Japanese people are generally enthusiastic about sharing their favorite eateries and food recommendations. Engaging in conversations with locals can lead you to off-the-beaten-path restaurants that may become the highlight of your trip.

Remember, dining in Japan is not just about the food—it's a cultural experience. Embrace the Japanese dining etiquette, show respect to the chefs and staff, and immerse yourself in the unique flavors and traditions of the country. With a sense of adventure and a willingness to explore, you will discover unforgettable culinary delights throughout your journey in Japan.

POPULAR LOCAL DISHES BY CITY

Our travel party ranged from seven to ten people at any given time, as we did meet up with some friends who live in Japan, and they decided to wander around with us. That was a benefit when it came time for dining out, as there were additional meals placed on the table that could be passed around so nearly everyone could get a taste. That's pretty much how we managed our meals, as we wanted to experience as many different foods as possible within the country, and we decided that to the best of our abilities, at every meal – every person would order something different, and it was a shared meal. What else should you do when traveling with friends and family?

Here's some of what we tasted and much we learned about Japanese food in each city throughout our trip.

Tokyo

> **Sushi.** Fresh and delicious sushi can be found in many sushi bars and restaurants throughout Tokyo.
>
> **Ramen.** Tokyo-style ramen is known for its flavorful broth and thin noodles.
>
> **Monjayaki.** A Tokyo specialty, monjayaki is a savory pancake made with various ingredients like cabbage, seafood, and meat.
>
> **Tempura.** Crispy and light tempura, typically made with seafood and vegetables, is a popular dish in Tokyo.
>
> **Tsukemen.** A variation of ramen, tsukemen features noodles served separately from a rich, flavorful dipping sauce.

Kyoto

> **Kaiseki Ryori.** Kyoto is famous for its traditional multi-course kaiseki meals, which consist of small, artfully prepared dishes that showcase seasonal ingredients.
>
> **Yudofu.** A simple and comforting dish, yudofu is a hot pot of tofu simmered in a light soy-based broth.
>
> **Matcha Sweets.** Kyoto is renowned for its matcha (green tea) desserts, including matcha ice cream, matcha-flavored cakes, and traditional tea ceremonies.

Obanzai. Kyoto-style home-cooked dishes made with local, seasonal ingredients, often served as small side dishes.

Saba-zushi. Kyoto-style sushi featuring pickled mackerel pressed onto vinegared rice.

Osaka

Okonomiyaki. A savory pancake with various ingredients such as cabbage, pork, seafood, and noodles, topped with a tangy sauce and mayonnaise.

Takoyaki. Osaka's famous street food, takoyaki are crispy, round balls filled with octopus and topped with various sauces and bonito flakes.

Kushikatsu. Skewered and deep-fried meat, seafood, and vegetables, typically served with a dipping sauce.

Kitsune Udon. Udon noodles served in a flavorful broth with sweetened deep-fried tofu (kitsune).

Negiyaki. A savory pancake similar to okonomiyaki, but with a stronger focus on the green onions (negi) as the main ingredient.

Hiroshima

Hiroshima-style Okonomiyaki. A variation of okonomiyaki, Hiroshima-style features layered ingredients, including cabbage, noodles, pork, and a fried egg, creating a unique and delicious dish.

Hiroshima-style Tsukemen. Thick and chewy ramen noodles served separately from a flavorful dipping broth.

Hiroshima-style Oysters. Hiroshima is known for its fresh and plump oysters, which can be grilled, fried, or in various other preparations.

Anago Meshi. Grilled conger eel served on a bed of rice, often with a sweet soy-based sauce.

Momiji Manju. A popular souvenir snack, momiji manju are small maple leaf-shaped cakes filled with sweet bean paste or other flavored fillings.

Kamakura

Shirasu Don. A bowl of rice topped with tiny, whitebait fish (shirasu), often served with various accompaniments like seaweed and pickled vegetables.

Shojin Ryori. Kamakura is home to several Zen temples, where you can experience shojin ryori, a vegetarian Buddhist cuisine known for its simplicity and emphasis on seasonal ingredients.

Kamakura Zenzai. A sweet red bean soup served with mochi (rice cake) or shiratama (glutinous rice dumplings).

Hato Sable. A popular Kamakura souvenir, hato sable are heart-shaped butter cookies with a rich and crumbly texture.

These are just a few examples of each city's delicious dishes and specialties. Enjoy exploring the local culinary delights!

FOOD FINDER RESOURCES

In our planning stages of the trip, we asked each person traveling to provide one online resource that each of us could visit to gather information about the culinary culture in Japan.

The resources we found with the best and most reliable information are listed below.

TripAdvisor. TripAdvisor is a well-known online platform that provides user-generated reviews and ratings for restaurants worldwide, including in Japan. It offers a vast selection of dining options, allowing you to browse through different categories, read reviews, and find highly recommended restaurants in various cities across Japan.

Tabelog. Tabelog is a comprehensive restaurant review and rating website focusing on Japan. It features a vast database of restaurants covering various cuisines and price ranges. Tabelog provides detailed information, including user reviews, photos, menus, and ratings, allowing you to make informed decisions when choosing a restaurant.

Michelin Guide. The Michelin Guide is renowned for its prestigious restaurant ratings and recommendations worldwide. In Japan, the Michelin Guide covers major cities like Tokyo, Kyoto, and Osaka, highlighting exceptional dining establishments. Michelin-starred restaurants are often associated with top-quality cuisine and unique culinary experiences.

Gurunavi. Gurunavi is a popular restaurant search platform that caters specifically to Japan. It offers a vast directory of restaurants, including high-end establishments and more casual options. Gurunavi provides comprehensive information such as menus, pricing, location details, and user reviews, helping you explore a wide range of dining experiences.

Local Food Blogs and Websites. Japan has a vibrant food blogging community, with numerous bloggers sharing their experiences and recommendations. Look for local food blogs and websites dedicated to Japanese cuisine, specific cities, or even niche food interests. These platforms often provide insightful articles, detailed restaurant reviews, and valuable tips for exploring the local food scene.

Food Tours and Experiences. Joining a food tour or culinary experience is an excellent way to discover hidden gems and experience authentic Japanese cuisine. Various tour companies offer guided food tours, walking tours, or cooking classes that provide insider knowledge and take you to local eateries and food markets.

Social Media Platforms. Platforms like Instagram and food-focused communities can be valuable resources for finding restaurant recommendations and food experiences in Japan. Follow food influencers, search for location-specific hashtags, and explore posts from fellow food enthusiasts to discover popular restaurants, unique dishes, and trending food spots. There are even Japanese food groups and pages on some social media platforms.

Finding the Best Restaurants in Japan can be a delightful adventure for food enthusiasts. Japanese cuisine is celebrated worldwide for its precision, attention to detail, and emphasis on fresh, seasonal ingredients.

Understanding Japanese dining etiquette and customs can enhance your dining experience. Familiarize yourself with traditions like saying "Itadakimasu" and using chopsticks properly before starting a meal. Japanese restaurants often specialize in specific types of cuisine, such as sushi, ramen, or izakaya (Japanese pubs), so be open to trying different dining styles.

In this chapter, we've covered a lot of great information to help you experience the extraordinary culinary scene in Japan. It is safe to say that it is likely no corner within the cities we cover in this book where you wouldn't be able to find a delicious treat. Remember that one of the best ways to discover great restaurants is by observing where the locals dine. Look for places with a queue or crowded with locals, often indicators of delicious food. Venture beyond tourist hotspots and explore residential neighborhoods to find hidden gems known only to the locals.

Each city in Japan has its culinary specialties that are not to be missed. In Tokyo, indulge in sushi at Tsukiji Fish Market or savor the delicate flavors of kaiseki (a traditional multi-course meal). Try matcha (green tea) sweets and kyo-kaiseki in Kyoto, a refined and elegant dining experience. Osaka is renowned for its street food, including takoyaki (octopus balls) and okonomiyaki (savory pancake). Hiroshima offers its unique style of okonomiyaki, while Kamakura is known for its delicious seafood.

Interacting with locals can provide valuable insights and recommendations. Contact hotel staff, taxi drivers, or friendly locals to discover their favorite dining spots. Join food tours or cooking classes led by knowledgeable guides who can introduce you to authentic and off-the-beaten-path culinary experiences.

Also, remember the best restaurants in Japan may not always be the most glamorous or well-known. Don't be afraid to explore small, family-run establishments or local food markets, as these can offer unforgettable dining experiences. Trust your instincts, be adventurous with your food choices, and savor the diverse flavors of Japan.

Bon appétit!

Inspire Others To Travel to Japan And Uncover Their Trip Of A Lifetime!

How familiar are you with the enchanting country of Japan? If your answer falls somewhere between "I don't know" and "not much" – you're not alone. While traditional bulky travel books may provide semi-valuable insights and many pages of filler, their focus often leaves the details of hidden gems like Tokyo, Kyoto, Osaka, Kamakura and Hiroshima largely undiscovered.

Embarking on a journey using "Travel Japan: Unveiling Culture, Language & Local Gems" not only immerses you in the beauty of Japan but guarantees a memorable adventure. However, the key to unlocking the full experience lies in having the right information at your fingertips. Drawing from my own planning and itinerary, my mission is to share insights that empower you to uncover the cultural richness and unforgettable memories of each city and design your own unforgettable itinerary using Travel Japan as a baseline.

Think about the countless travel enthusiasts navigating the vast array of options, just like you. Your assistance in spreading the word about this travel guide can make a world of difference, and it requires so little time—less than a few minutes, all from the comfort of your own home!

The secret to passing along this invaluable guidance is as straightforward as sharing a brief review online. By expressing your thoughts about "Travel Japan" on platforms like Amazon, you're helping other wanderlust-stricken travelers stumble upon this wealth of information about Japan's hidden treasures.

The power of book reviews cannot be overstated!

Honest book reviews are the validation providing us with the answers to our questions. A simple few sentences written by you could inspire a fellow traveler to navigate Japan's diverse landscapes and cultural wonders using "Travel Japan" as a roadmap, much as you chose to do.

By leaving a review of "Travel Japan" on Amazon, you'll ensure other explorers find this book, and discover the full array of possibilities for their once-in-a-lifetime trip to Japan.

Your support is the validation that will inspire and educate travelers in similar planning stages to yours.

Take a moment to leave a book review, and after that, let's continue on this journey toward Japanese cultural discovery and unforgettable experiences!

Your voice matters more than you think!

Scan the QR code to write a sentence or two and leave an honest Amazon review that will inspire fellow travelers!.

6

LODGING IN JAPAN

PRIVATE RENTALS

When planning a trip to Japan, one of the crucial aspects to consider is lodging. While hotels are popular, an alternative option gaining popularity is renting accommodations through vacation rental platforms like VRBO (Vacation Rentals By Owner) or Airbnb. This subtopic explores the costs associated with renting properties through these platforms in four prominent cities of Japan: Tokyo, Kyoto, Osaka, and Hiroshima. Understanding the rental costs and factors influencing them can help travelers budget effectively and make informed decisions.

Assessing VRBOs and Airbnb for travelers is an important aspect of planning your stay in Japan. Here's a closer look at the key points to consider when choosing a VRBO, Airbnb, or alternative accommodation options.

Staying in private rentals can offer several advantages. First, they often provide more space and amenities than traditional hotel rooms, making them suitable for families or travelers who desire a home-like environment. Second, private rentals can be more cost-effective, especially for longer stays, as they generally have lower nightly rates than hotels. Additionally, staying in a residential neighborhood can provide a unique and authentic experience, allowing you to immerse yourself in the local culture.

However, there are some cons to be aware of. Private rentals may not offer the same level of service and security as hotels. For example, you won't have access to daily housekeeping, concierge services, or on-site staff for immediate assistance. Additionally, not all private rentals meet the same quality standards, and there is a possibility of encountering issues such as misrepresentation, cleanliness concerns, or lack of amenities. It's crucial to thoroughly assess each listing before making a reservation.

When choosing a private rental, consider location, budget, and amenities. Consider what you prioritize regarding proximity to public transportation, attractions, or specific neighborhoods. Determine your budget and search for accommodations within your price range. Assess amenities like Wi-Fi, kitchen facilities, laundry, and parking, to ensure they align with your needs and preferences.

Reading reviews from previous guests is essential in assessing the quality and reliability of a private rental listing. Pay attention to the overall rating, comments about cleanliness, the accuracy of the listing description, and communication with the host. Take note of any recurring issues or concerns mentioned in the reviews, as they can give you valuable insights into the property and the host's responsiveness.

Communication with hosts is crucial for a smooth rental experience. Reach out to the host before making a reservation to clarify any questions or special requests you may have.

Ensure you understand the house rules, check-in procedures, and any additional fees. Clear and prompt communication with the host can help address any potential issues or uncertainties upfront.

Remember that Airbnb or VRBO is not the only option for accommodation. Consider alternative options such as traditional hotels, guesthouses, ryokans (traditional Japanese inns), or capsule hotels. Each option offers a different experience and level of comfort, so it's worth exploring all possibilities to find the best fit for your travel preferences and budget.

Rental costs for VRBO and Airbnb properties in Japan vary depending on several factors, including location, size, amenities, and demand. Tokyo, the bustling capital city, generally has higher rental prices than other cities. The high demand for accommodations, the city's vibrant urban atmosphere, and international appeal contribute to higher prices. Kyoto, known for its rich history and traditional charm, also sees significant demand for vacation rentals. While prices can be lower than in Tokyo, they are still relatively higher due to the city's cultural significance and tourist popularity. Osaka, a vibrant metropolis renowned for its food scene and entertainment, offers more diverse rental options. The city's competitive market can lead to a wider price range, with affordable options available alongside more expensive choices. Rental costs in Osaka often reflect factors such as location, size, and amenities. Despite its historical significance, Hiroshima generally offers more affordable rental options than other cities. The city's relative affordability can be attributed to factors such as its location outside the primary tourist circuits and the availability of a wider range of accommodations.

By considering the pros and cons of staying in a private rental, carefully assessing listings and reviews, and maintaining good communication with hosts, you can make an informed decision and find suitable accommodation that enhances your travel experience in Japan.

Many of the private rentals in Japan are full-time rentals. Therefore, their owners take great pride in providing the best accommodations at an affordable price. Throughout our journey to the five cities, we stayed in three private rentals and one hotel the night before our departure. It was a convenient hotel due to its proximity to the airport and the short 30-second train ride to the Haneda airport station.

JAPANESE HOMES

The traditional Japanese home has multiple sleeping rooms and two to three residential floors. The typical home and private rentals in Japan can be found with many of these types of rooms:

> **Genkan (Entrance Hall).** The genkan is a small sunken area at the house's entrance where shoes are removed before stepping into the main living area.
>
> **Washitsu (Japanese-style Room).** A washitsu is a traditional Japanese-style room with tatami flooring and sliding doors called fusuma. This room is often used for various purposes like dining, entertaining guests, or as a sleeping area.
>
> **Zashiki (Reception Room).** A zashiki is a formal reception room typically found in larger houses. It is often used for hosting guests or tea ceremonies and may feature a raised alcove called a tokonoma for displaying art or decorations.

Kitchens. In modern Japanese houses, kitchens are often Western-style, with standard appliances like stovetops, ovens, and refrigerators. However, some traditional houses may still have a separate washoku (Japanese-style kitchen) where traditional cooking methods and utensils are used.

Bedrooms. Bedrooms in Japanese houses can vary in size and style. Some houses may have individual bedrooms for each family member, while others may have shared sleeping areas with futons on tatami mats. In more modern homes, bedrooms may be furnished with Western-style beds.

Water Closet. The water closet, or toilet, is usually found in a separate room from the bathing area. Japanese toilets often feature advanced features like bidet functions, heated seats, and automatic flushing.

Ofuro (Bathing Area). The ofuro is the bathing area in a Japanese house. It typically consists of a deep soaking tub, often made of wood, and a shower or bathing area. In traditional houses, the ofuro may be a separate room; in modern houses, it may be combined with the toilet area.

Engawa (Veranda). The engawa is an enclosed or semi-enclosed veranda that surrounds the house. It serves as a transitional space between the interior and the exterior and can be used for relaxation or as an additional seating area.

Fusuma and Shoji Screens. Some accommodations feature sliding doors called fusuma and shoji screens, iconic Japanese architectural elements. These screens are used to divide rooms and create flexible spaces. Fusuma often have decorative elements or paintings, while shoji screens are made of translucent paper, allowing natural light to filter through.

Zen Elements. Many traditional Japanese rentals incorporate Zen elements such as Zen gardens, meditation spaces, or mini rock gardens (karesansui). These features contribute to a serene atmosphere, promoting relaxation and a sense of mindfulness.

AMENITIES AND LOCATION

The amenities offered and the rental property's location are significant in determining the rental costs. Properties with desirable amenities like Wi-Fi, air conditioning, fully equipped kitchens, and proximity to popular attractions tend to command higher prices. Additionally, accommodations in prime locations, such as near major train stations or sought-after neighborhoods, often come at a premium. Travelers seeking budget-friendly options might find accommodations far from city centers or popular tourist areas. While these properties could offer more competitive prices, it is essential to consider the convenience and additional transportation costs associated with a more distant location.

Understanding the rental costs for VRBO and Airbnb properties in Tokyo, Kyoto, Osaka, and Hiroshima is crucial when planning a trip to Japan. Travelers should be prepared for higher rental prices in Tokyo and Kyoto due to the cities' popularity and demand. Osaka provides a more diverse range of options, while Hiroshima generally offers more affordable choices. Amenities and location are significant factors influencing rental costs, with properties boasting desirable amenities and prime locations commanding higher prices. By considering these factors, travelers can budget effectively and select accommodations that suit their preferences and financial means during their stay in Japan.

It's also important to note that the availability of specific amenities may vary from one rental to another. However, these amenities commonly found in traditional Japanese rentals help create an authentic and immersive experience, allowing guests to appreciate and engage with Japanese culture and traditions during their stay.

As we've learned, the options for lodging in Japan have a few distinct variables, with some commonalities as well. The best-suggested method to secure your lodging is visiting the online private rental websites and sorting by your intended overnight locations. Many of the listed Japanese rentals on these websites can seemingly accommodate seven to ten people very easily, as many private rentals have multiple Washitsu or bedrooms to sleep a large travel party. Purveyors of Japanese private rentals are very communicative and provide all the information needed to ensure your stay in their homes. Additionally, it's not uncommon to find a rental homeowner or a rental host that will help their guests arrange reservations at restaurants, provide English-written guides to attractions or train stations, and even offer to meet you at the rental upon check-in to ensure your stay will be pleasant and to answer any questions about the features of the rental that you may not be able to understand.

7

WEATHER IN THE FIVE CITIES

As travelers journey through Japan, they are greeted by a tapestry of weather patterns and atmospheric nuances in the five captivating cities of Tokyo, Osaka, Kamakura, Kyoto, and Hiroshima. Each city boasts a different distinct climate, offering a unique experience for visitors. From the bustling streets of Tokyo, where summers can be hot and humid, to the vibrant energy of Osaka with its mild winters, the coastal charm of Kamakura with refreshing sea breezes, the serene beauty of Kyoto defined by its changing seasons, to the historical significance of Hiroshima with its temperate climate, the weather in these cities provides a diverse backdrop to the rich cultural tapestry that awaits exploration. In this chapter, we delve into the brief differences in weather that define these extraordinary cities, allowing travelers to prepare for and embrace the atmospheric nuances they will encounter on their journey through Japan.

TOKYO

Tokyo experiences a humid subtropical climate with distinct seasons. Spring (March to May) brings mild temperatures and the iconic cherry blossoms. Summers (June to August) are hot and humid with occasional rain showers. Autumn (September to November) is mild and pleasant with colorful foliage. Winters (December to February) are cool but rarely extremely cold. Typhoons may occur during the summer and early autumn months.

When packing for Tokyo, consider the season. In spring, pack lightweight and breathable clothing as temperatures gradually rise. Summer calls for light, airy clothing, sunscreen, and an umbrella for sudden rain showers. Autumn requires layers to accommodate cool mornings and evenings. Winter necessitates warm clothing, including a coat, hat, gloves, and a scarf.

Various festivals and events take place throughout the year in Tokyo. Some notable ones include the Tokyo Marathon (March), Cherry Blossom Festival (late March to early April), Sumida River Fireworks (July), Kanda Matsuri (May, odd-numbered years), and Tokyo International Film Festival (October).

Tokyo, the vibrant capital of Japan, experiences a humid subtropical climate with distinct seasons. Spring, from March to May, is a delightful time to visit Tokyo. The temperatures are mild, ranging from around 10°C (50°F) to 20°C (68°F), and the city becomes adorned with beautiful cherry blossoms. Parks and gardens, such as Ueno Park and Shinjuku Gyoen, have become popular hanami (flower viewing) spots as locals and tourists gather to appreciate the delicate pink blossoms.

From June to August, summers in Tokyo can be hot and humid. Temperatures often soar above 30°C (86°F), accompanied by high humidity. It's important to stay hydrated and seek shade during this time. Tokyo's summer also brings occasional rain showers, so carrying an umbrella or raincoat is a good idea. Despite the heat, the city remains bustling with activity, and you can enjoy various outdoor festivals and events.

Autumn, from September to November, is another pleasant season in Tokyo. The temperatures become milder, ranging from around 15°C (59°F) to 25°C (77°F), and the cityscape transforms into a colorful tapestry as the leaves change into vibrant hues of red, orange, and gold. Parks like Yoyogi Park and Rikugien Garden offer picturesque settings for autumn strolls and picnics. It's an excellent time to explore the city's many attractions without the sweltering heat of summer.

Winters in Tokyo, from December to February, are relatively mild compared to other regions in Japan. The temperatures range from around 5°C (41°F) to 15°C (59°F), with occasional cold spells. While snowfall is infrequent, you may experience some chilly days. Dressing in layers and carrying a warm jacket or coat is advisable. Winter in Tokyo has its own charm, with stunning illuminations decorating the city streets and seasonal events such as the New Year's celebrations at shrines and temples.

Typhoons, tropical cyclones that bring strong winds and heavy rain, can occur in Tokyo during the summer and early autumn. While they are a natural occurrence, it's essential to stay updated on weather forecasts and follow any instructions or advisories from local authorities. Tokyo's infrastructure is well-prepared for such situations, but it's wise to be aware and take necessary precautions if a typhoon is expected during your visit.

KYOTO

Kyoto has a similar climate to Tokyo, characterized by four distinct seasons. Spring and autumn are particularly beautiful in Kyoto, attracting many visitors. Summers can be hot and humid, while winters are generally cold but milder than in other parts of Japan.

Consider the season and the city's cultural significance when packing for Kyoto. In spring, pack lightweight clothing for cherry blossom viewing. Summers call for light and breathable clothing, sunscreen, and a hat. Autumn requires layers to accommodate fluctuating temperatures and vibrant foliage. Winter necessitates warm clothing, including a coat, hat, gloves, and a scarf. Kyoto hosts several festivals and events, including the famous Gion Matsuri (July), Hanatouro (March), Aoi Matsuri (May), and Jidai Matsuri (October). These events offer a glimpse into Kyoto's rich cultural heritage.

Kyoto, the cultural heart of Japan, shares a climate similar to Tokyo's, featuring four distinct seasons. Spring and autumn are especially enchanting in Kyoto, making it a popular destination for travelers seeking natural beauty and cultural experiences. In spring, from March to May, the city bursts into a symphony of colors as cherry blossoms blanket parks and temples. The temperatures during this time range from around 10°C (50°F) to 20°C (68°F), creating a pleasant atmosphere for exploring the historic streets and gardens.

Between June and August, summers in Kyoto can be hot and humid, with temperatures often exceeding 30°C (86°F). It's advisable to dress in light and breathable clothing, stay hydrated, and take breaks in shaded or air-conditioned spaces. Despite the heat, Kyoto's allure remains intact, and you can immerse yourself in traditional cultural events, such as the Gion

Matsuri festival, where grand processions of floats parade through the streets.

A typical Kyoto Winter from December to February brings cooler temperatures and occasionally cold spells. While the city rarely sees heavy snowfall, temperatures can drop to around 0°C (32°F) on colder days. It's recommended to bundle up in warm layers and bring a winter coat, especially if you plan to explore temples and gardens. The serene atmosphere of Kyoto during winter creates a unique ambiance, and you can experience traditional winter festivals like To-ji Temple's illumination or enjoy a hot bowl of yudofu (tofu hot pot) to warm yourself from within.

Autumn, from September to November, is another enchanting season in Kyoto. The city becomes adorned with the breathtaking colors of autumn foliage, known as koyo. Parks and temples like Kiyomizu-dera and Arashiyama's bamboo forest become popular destinations for appreciating the leaves' vibrant reds, oranges, and yellows. The temperatures during this time range from around 10°C (50°F) to 20°C (68°F), providing a comfortable climate for exploring the city's cultural treasures.

Kyoto's climate throughout the year offers travelers a diverse range of experiences. Whether it's witnessing the cherry blossoms in spring, escaping the summer heat in serene temples, embracing the winter charm of illuminated gardens, or reveling in the autumn colors, Kyoto promises an unforgettable journey through its seasons.

OSAKA

Osaka has a similar climate to Tokyo and Kyoto, with mild winters and hot, humid summers. Spring and autumn are pleasant seasons to visit.

Consider the season and the city's vibrant atmosphere when packing for Osaka. In spring, pack lightweight clothing for cherry blossom viewing. Summers call for light and breathable clothing, sunscreen, and an umbrella for sudden rain showers. Autumn requires layers to accommodate cool mornings and evenings. Winter requirements for warm clothing include a coat, hat, gloves, and scarf.

Like Tokyo and Kyoto, Osaka experiences a climate similar to that of Kyoto, characterized by distinct seasons. Spring and autumn are particularly pleasant seasons to visit this vibrant city. From March to May, Osaka comes alive in spring with cherry blossoms, creating picturesque scenes in parks and along riverbanks. The temperatures during this time range from around 10°C (50°F) to 20°C (68°F), making it comfortable for exploring the city's attractions and enjoying outdoor activities.

Osaka Summers can be hot and humid from June to August, often exceeding 30°C (86°F). It's important to dress in light and breathable clothing, stay hydrated, and seek shade or air-conditioned spaces when needed. Despite the heat, Osaka's energetic atmosphere continues to thrive, and you can indulge in the city's vibrant street food scene, visit iconic landmarks like Osaka Castle, or enjoy summer festivals such as the Tenjin Festival with its spectacular boat procession on the Okawa River.

Winter in Osaka, from December to February, brings cooler temperatures, but the city rarely experiences extreme cold. It's advisable to pack warm clothing, including a coat, hat, gloves, and a scarf, as temperatures can drop to around 0°C (32°F) on colder days. During this season, you can experience the festive atmosphere of Osaka, visit illuminated displays, and savor delicious winter specialties like hot pot dishes and grilled street food.

Throughout the year, Osaka hosts various festivals and events that showcase the city's lively and celebratory spirit. The Tenjin Festival in July is one of the most renowned festivals in Japan, featuring processions, traditional performances, and fireworks. The Osaka Castle Park Cherry Blossom Festival in April is a delightful time to witness the blooming cherry blossoms while enjoying food stalls and cultural performances. The Sumiyoshi Taisha Grand Festival in July is another notable event with colorful processions and traditional rituals at Sumiyoshi Taisha, one of Osaka's most important shrines.

Osaka's climate and vibrant atmosphere offer travelers a range of experiences throughout the year. Whether strolling through cherry blossom-lined streets in spring, indulging in summer festivals, embracing the charm of winter illuminations, or savoring the city's culinary delights, Osaka promises a dynamic and memorable journey.

HIROSHIMA

Hiroshima has a mild climate, with hot summers and mild winters. Spring and autumn are particularly pleasant seasons to visit, offering comfortable temperatures.

When choosing appropriate clothing for Hiroshima, consider the season and the city's historical significance. In spring, pack lightweight clothing for cherry blossom viewing. Summers call for light and breathable clothing, sunscreen, and an umbrella for sudden rain showers. Autumn requires layers to accommodate cool mornings and evenings. Winter necessitates warm clothing, including a coat, hat, gloves, and a scarf.

Hiroshima hosts the Hiroshima Peace Memorial Ceremony (August 6) to commemorate the atomic bombing and promote peace. Popular events include the Hiroshima Flower Festival (May) and the Miyajima Water Fireworks Festival (August).

During spring, from March to May, Hiroshima bursts into color as cherry blossoms bloom across the city. It's a magical time to visit the Peace Memorial Park and enjoy hanami (flower viewing) picnics under the cherry trees. The temperatures range from around 10°C (50°F) to 20°C (68°F), making it ideal for outdoor exploration.

From June to August, Summers in Hiroshima can be hot and humid, with temperatures often reaching 30°C (86°F) or higher. Packing light and breathable clothing, sunscreen, a hat, and an umbrella for sudden rain showers is advisable. Despite the heat, Hiroshima holds significant events during this season, such as the Hiroshima Peace Memorial Ceremony on August 6. This solemn ceremony commemorates the atomic bombing of the city and promotes peace and nuclear disarmament.

Autumn, from September to November, brings comfortable temperatures and vibrant foliage. It's a beautiful time to visit Hiroshima's parks and gardens, including the Shukkeien Garden and Miyajima Island. The temperatures range from around 15°C (59°F) to 25°C (77°F), making it pleasant for sightseeing and outdoor activities. Layered clothing is recommended to accommodate cool mornings and evenings.

In Hiroshima, Winter (December to February) is relatively mild but can still bring cooler temperatures—average temperatures during this season range from 5°C to 12°C (41°F to 54°F). While snowfall is rare, occasional chilly days can occur, so it's advisable to pack a warm coat or jacket to stay comfortable. Winter layering is key in Hiroshima, as indoor spaces may be heated while outdoor temperatures can be cooler. Pack long-sleeved shirts, sweaters, and thermal layers to provide warmth when needed. Additionally, include pants, jeans, or skirts, and don't forget to pack warm socks and closed-toe shoes or boots to keep your feet cozy. Accessories such as gloves, hats, scarves, and earmuffs are recommended to protect yourself from the cold, especially during colder days or when venturing out in the evenings. An umbrella or a compact raincoat is also a good idea, as winter in Hiroshima can bring occasional rainfall.

Hiroshima is known for its lively festivals and events showcasing its culture and traditions. The Hiroshima Flower Festival in May celebrates the arrival of spring with parades, music performances, and food stalls. In August, the Miyajima Water Fireworks Festival is a stunning spectacle where fireworks are launched over the water, creating a magical display. These events give visitors a deeper understanding of Hiroshima's vibrant spirit and commitment to promoting peace and resilience.

The mild climate in Hiroshima, beautiful seasons, and significant events make it a captivating destination year-round. Whether you're marveling at cherry blossoms in spring, commemorating the past during the Peace Memorial Ceremony yearly on August 6th, enjoying the colors of autumn foliage, or immersing yourself in the vibrant atmosphere of local festivals, Hiroshima offers a unique and memorable travel experience.

KAMAKURA

Kamakura, nestled along Japan's picturesque coast, is a city of cultural significance and natural beauty. Its maritime climate, influenced by the nearby Pacific Ocean, creates pleasant and temperate weather throughout the year. When packing for a trip to Kamakura, it's important to consider the varying weather conditions and the typical seasonal patterns.

Springtime is March to May in Kamakura and is a delightful time to visit as temperatures gradually rise and nature bursts into life. Cherry blossoms, an iconic symbol of Japan, painted the city with delicate pink hues in late March and early April. The weather during this season is generally mild, with temperatures ranging from 10°C to 20°C (50°F to 68°F). It's advisable to pack layered clothing, including light sweaters and jackets, as mornings and evenings can still be cool.

Summer lasts from June to August in Kamakura, bringing warmer temperatures and higher humidity. Average temperatures range from 20°C to 30°C (68°F to 86°F). Pack lightweight and breathable clothing, such as shorts, T-shirts, and summer dresses, is important. Don't forget essentials like sunscreen, a hat, and insect repellent, as you'll likely spend time exploring the city's outdoor attractions and beaches. Although rain is less frequent during summer, having a foldable umbrella or a raincoat handy is advisable, as occasional showers can occur.

Autumn in Kamakura (September to November) is a season of beauty as the leaves change color, creating a captivating backdrop for sightseeing. Temperatures become milder, ranging from 15°C to 25°C (59°F to 77°F). Layering clothing is still recommended, as mornings and evenings can be cooler while afternoons are pleasant. Pack a light jacket or sweater to stay comfortable during temperature fluctuations. Autumn is also a relatively dry season, so you can leave the umbrella behind and focus on enjoying the stunning fall foliage.

Kamakura has a Winter season of December to February and has cooler temperatures, although it remains relatively mild compared to other regions of Japan. Average temperatures range from 5°C to 15°C (41°F to 59°F). While snowfall is infrequent, it's still a good idea to pack a warm coat, gloves, a hat, and scarves for colder days. Layering is essential during this season, as indoor spaces may be heated, while outdoor temperatures can be chilly.

When visiting Kamakura, it's advisable to pack clothing suitable for layering, comfortable walking shoes, and appropriate seasonal accessories. Remember to check the local weather forecast before your trip and adjust your packing accordingly. Whether strolling along Kamakura's historical sites, exploring its beautiful coastline, or immersing yourself in its cultural treasures, preparing for the weather ensures a more enjoyable and comfortable experience in this enchanting city.

TOP ATTRACTIONS

Welcome to the exciting world of Japan's most captivating and bustling cities! This chapter will explore some of the most notable free and low-cost attractions within Tokyo, Osaka, Kyoto, Hiroshima, and Kamakura.

Embark on our adventure in Tokyo, a city that blends modernity with the charm of the past. Begin by exploring the famous Shibuya Crossing, where thousands of pedestrians harmoniously come together and marvel at Shinjuku's dazzling lights and vibrant atmosphere, known for its towering skyscrapers, lively nightlife, and exceptional shopping opportunities. Take a moment to immerse yourself in the tranquil beauty of the Meiji Shrine, nestled in a serene forest, and satisfy your curiosity by delving into the captivating history and remarkable art collections at the Tokyo National Museum. Experience the futuristic architecture of the Tokyo Skytree and be transported back in time as you appreciate the historical allure of Asakusa's Senso-ji Temple and the centuries-old Tokyo Imperial Palace. The attractions in Tokyo are a remarkable fusion of history and modernity, taking you on a captivating trip through time.

Next, we venture to Osaka, renowned for its culinary delights and lively atmosphere. Indulge in mouthwatering street food at Dotonbori, where sizzling takoyaki and savory okonomiyaki tempt your taste buds. Marvel at the grandeur of Osaka Castle, a magnificent fortress that stands as a testament to Japan's feudal past, and immerse yourself in the vibrant atmosphere of the bustling Namba district. Discover the wonders of Universal Studios Japan, where thrilling rides and beloved movie characters come to life, or wander through the tranquil beauty of the Osaka Mint Bureau's cherry blossom-lined streets during spring.

Our trip then takes us to Kyoto, a city steeped in ancient traditions and cultural treasures. Lose yourself in the mesmerizing beauty of the Golden Pavilion (Kinkaku-ji), a shimmering temple set amidst a stunning garden landscape. Experience the peaceful ambiance of the iconic Arashiyama Bamboo Grove and explore the historic district of Gion, where geisha culture thrives. Kyoto's wealth of UNESCO World Heritage Sites, including the magnificent Kiyomizu-dera and the serene Ryoan-ji Temple, make it an unforgettable destination for those seeking an authentic glimpse into Japan's rich heritage.

In Osaka, embrace the energetic spirit of Japan's second-largest city. Discover the vibrant Dotonbori district, famous for its neon lights, bustling streets, and delectable street food. Immerse yourself in the historical ambiance of Osaka Castle, a magnificent fortress with a rich heritage. Indulge in the vibrant atmosphere of the Umeda Sky Building, offering breathtaking panoramic views of the cityscape. Explore Namba's vibrant shopping and entertainment district, filled with shops, restaurants, and theaters. Osaka's cultural treasures, such as the Osaka Museum of History and the Shitennoji Temple, provide insights into the city's past and traditions.

As we travel further, we arrive in Hiroshima, a city that stands as a symbol of resilience and peace. Visit the Hiroshima Peace Memorial Park, a poignant reminder of the city's tragic past, and pay tribute to the victims of the atomic bombing at the Hiroshima Peace Memorial Museum. Take a tranquil stroll through the picturesque Hiroshima Castle and enjoy the beauty of Shukkei-en Garden, a meticulously landscaped oasis of calm. Hiroshima's transformation into a vibrant, thriving city is a testament to the indomitable spirit of its people.

Finally, we go to Kamakura, a coastal gem known for its rich history and serene beauty. Marvel at the Great Buddha of Kamakura, a towering bronze statue that has watched over the city for centuries. Explore the enchanting Tsurugaoka Hachimangu Shrine, where ancient rituals and traditions continue to thrive, and venture to the scenic shores of Yuigahama Beach. Kamakura's temples, quaint streets, and breathtaking natural landscapes make it a delightful retreat from the bustling cities of Japan.

Join us as we delve into the must-visit attractions that define the essence of these captivating cities. Your exploration of Japan will Prepare you to be enthralled by the endless possibilities in this unforgettable journey through Japan's most alluring destinations. From the modern marvels of Tokyo to the cultural gems of Kyoto, the historic significance of Hiroshima, and the coastal beauty of Kamakura, each city has its unique charm, ensuring a travel experience that will leave you with memories of your travels within this endearing country.

Although this book could have multiple chapters related to the large volume of tourist opportunities while traveling through

Japan, we've included some of the most notable free and low-cost attractions below. We've also included some attractions outside of the five major cities we've covered in this book as those attractions are easily accessible as a day trip.

TOKYO

Tokyo Disneyland. Tokyo Disneyland is a magical theme park that offers a unique Japanese twist on the classic Disney experience. Explore themed lands, enjoy thrilling rides, meet beloved Disney characters, and witness spectacular parades and shows. It's a must-visit attraction for families and Disney enthusiasts.

Meiji Shrine. Located in the heart of Tokyo, Meiji Shrine is a tranquil oasis amidst the bustling city. Dedicated to Emperor Meiji and Empress Shoken, a lush forest surrounds the shrine and features impressive torii gates, serene gardens, and traditional architecture. Take a peaceful stroll and experience a sense of serenity and spirituality.

Tsukiji Fish Market. As one of the world's largest fish markets, Tsukiji offers a vibrant and bustling atmosphere. Explore the outer market, where you can find an incredible array of fresh seafood, local produce, and kitchenware. Don't miss the opportunity to savor delicious sushi at the market's renowned sushi restaurants.

Shibuya Crossing. Experience the iconic Shibuya Crossing, often called the busiest intersection in the world. Watch as a sea of pedestrians crisscross the streets from multiple directions when the traffic lights turn red. Capture the energy of this famous landmark and explore the vibrant shopping and entertainment district surrounding it.

Tokyo Skytree. Towering over the city skyline, Tokyo Skytree is a modern architectural marvel and a must-visit attraction for panoramic views of Tokyo. Take the elevator to the observation decks at different heights, and enjoy breathtaking city vistas and beyond. The Skytree also houses various shops, restaurants, and entertainment facilities.

Nikko. Located a few hours from Tokyo, Nikko is a UNESCO World Heritage site known for its stunning shrines and natural beauty. Visit Toshogu Shrine, explore the picturesque Lake Chuzenji, and marvel at the Kegon Falls. Nikko offers a serene escape from the city and a glimpse into Japan's rich history.

Kamakura. Just a short train ride from Tokyo, Kamakura is a charming coastal town with many cultural and historical treasures. Visit the iconic Great Buddha at Kotoku-in Temple, explore the picturesque Hase-dera Temple, and enjoy the beautiful beaches and coastal scenery. Kamakura offers a peaceful retreat with a blend of nature and spirituality.

Yokohama. Located south of Tokyo, Yokohama is a vibrant city with a captivating waterfront and a mix of modern and historical attractions. Explore the scenic Minato Mirai district, visit the historic Yokohama Chinatown, and enjoy panoramic views from the Landmark Tower Sky Garden. Don't miss the unique Cup Noodles Museum for a quirky and interactive experience.

Mount Takao. Escape the city and venture to Mount Takao, a popular hiking spot just outside Tokyo. The mountain offers several hiking trails suitable for various fitness levels, leading to the summit, where you can enjoy panoramic views of the surrounding landscape. Explore the tranquil temples along the way and savor delicious local cuisine at the mountain's base.

Hakone. Experience natural hot springs, stunning views of Mount Fuji, and traditional Ryokan accommodations in Hakone, a resort town near Tokyo. Take a scenic boat ride on Lake Ashi, ride the Hakone Ropeway for breathtaking vistas, and relax in the healing waters of the hot springs. Hakone offers a perfect combination of relaxation and natural beauty.

KYOTO

Kiyomizu-dera Temple. Kiyomizu-dera is one of Kyoto's most iconic temples, known for its wooden terrace that offers stunning city views. Explore the temple's beautiful grounds, admire the traditional architecture, and immerse yourself in the serene atmosphere. Don't miss the opportunity to visit during cherry blossom or autumn when the surrounding trees are ablaze with vibrant colors.

Fushimi Inari Taisha. Fushimi Inari Taisha is a Shinto shrine famous for its thousands of vibrant red torii gates forming a mesmerizing mountain pathway. Take a leisurely hike through the gates and explore the peaceful forested trails. The shrine is dedicated to Inari, the Shinto god of rice and prosperity, and offers a unique spiritual experience.

Arashiyama Bamboo Grove. Step into a fairytale-like setting at the Arashiyama Bamboo Grove. Walk along the enchanting bamboo pathway, with towering bamboo stalks creating a tranquil and awe-inspiring atmosphere. Explore the surrounding area, including the beautiful Togetsukyo Bridge and the scenic Arashiyama Monkey Park.

Kinkaku-ji Temple. Known as the Golden Pavilion, Kinkaku-ji is a stunning Zen Buddhist temple adorned with gold leaf. Explore the meticulously manicured gardens and enjoy the temple's reflection in the peaceful pond. The temple's exquisite beauty and serene surroundings make it a must-visit attraction in Kyoto.

Gion District. Experience the charm of traditional Japan in the historic Gion district. Known as the geisha district, Gion is lined with narrow streets, traditional wooden machiya houses, and exclusive teahouses. Stroll through the district in the evening to catch a glimpse of geisha or maiko (apprentice geisha) gracefully making their way to engagements.

Nara. Just a short train ride from Kyoto, Nara is home to ancient temples, friendly deer roaming freely in Nara Park, and the awe-inspiring Great Buddha at Todai-ji Temple. Explore the tranquil gardens of Isuien and Yoshikien, and immerse yourself in the rich cultural heritage of Japan's first permanent capital.

Kiyomizu-Gojo Station. Take a short trip to Kiyomizu-Gojo Station just outside Kyoto and visit the enchanting Sanjusangendo Temple. Marvel at the temple's 1,001 statues of Kannon, the Buddhist goddess of mercy, and soak in the spiritual ambiance of this extraordinary place.

Fushimi Sake District. Discover the sake-making traditions of Kyoto at the Fushimi Sake District. Visit traditional breweries, learn about brewing, and enjoy sake-tasting experiences. Don't forget to explore the picturesque streets lined with traditional machiya houses and sample local delicacies.

Kibune and Kurama. Embark on a day trip to Kibune and Kurama, two charming villages in the mountains north of Kyoto. Enjoy a serene hike along the Kibune-Kurama Trail, visit the Kurama-dera Temple, and indulge in a relaxing hot spring bath at one of the village's traditional ryokans.

Higashiyama District. Immerse yourself in Kyoto's history and traditional atmosphere in the Higashiyama District. Explore narrow streets lined with traditional shops, visit historic temples such as Kiyomizu-dera and Yasaka Shrine, and sample local street food along the way.

OSAKA

Osaka Castle. A visit to Osaka is incomplete without exploring the iconic Osaka Castle. Immerse yourself in history as you explore the castle's majestic architecture and panoramic views from the top. The surrounding Osaka Castle Park is perfect for a stroll or a picnic amidst lush greenery.

Dotonbori. Experience the vibrant energy of Osaka at Dotonbori, a bustling street in the Namba district. Indulge in local street food, shop for quirky souvenirs, and admire the dazzling neon lights that line the canal. Don't miss the famous Glico Running Man sign and the lively atmosphere of this popular entertainment area.

Universal Studios Japan. For a dose of excitement and entertainment, head to Universal Studios Japan. Explore thrilling rides based on popular movies, catch live performances, and encounter beloved characters. From The Wizarding World of Harry Potter to Jurassic Park, this theme park offers fun for visitors of all ages.

Osaka Aquarium Kaiyukan. Explore the fascinating underwater world at Osaka Aquarium Kaiyukan, one of the largest aquariums in the world. Discover various marine life, including whale sharks, penguins, and otters. The highlight is the enormous central tank, which simulates the Pacific Ocean and houses diverse species.

Shinsaibashi and America-mura. Shopaholics will delight in the lively shopping districts of Shinsaibashi and America-mura.

Browse trendy boutiques, find unique fashion items, and explore the vibrant street art scene. These areas are perfect for people-watching, trying delicious street food, and embracing Osaka's fashionable and youthful culture.

Kobe. Experience a blend of history, culture, and delicious cuisine in the charming city of Kobe. Visit the iconic Kobe Harborland, explore the vibrant Chinatown, and savor the world-famous Kobe beef. Take a scenic ride on the Shin-Kobe Ropeway for breathtaking views of the city and the surrounding mountains.

Osaka Bay Area. Discover modern attractions in the Osaka Bay Area, including the popular Tempozan Ferris Wheel and the fascinating Osaka Aquarium Kaiyukan. Enjoy shopping and entertainment at the expansive Tempozan Marketplace, and take a relaxing cruise on the Santa Maria ship for a different perspective of Osaka's skyline.

Minoo Park. Escape the city and immerse yourself in nature at Minoo Park, just outside Osaka. Take a scenic hike through lush forests, visit the stunning Minoo Waterfall, and enjoy the tranquil atmosphere. The park is especially beautiful in autumn when the foliage turns vibrant shades of red and orange.

Osaka Museum of History. Dive into Osaka's rich history at the Osaka Museum of History near Osaka Castle. Explore interactive exhibits and displays that showcase the city's evolution from ancient times to the present. Gain insights into Osaka's culture, traditions, and significant historical events.

HIROSHIMA

Hiroshima Peace Memorial Park. A visit to Hiroshima is synonymous with a trip to the Hiroshima Peace Memorial

Park, a solemn and reflective space dedicated to the victims of the atomic bombing in 1945. Explore the Peace Memorial Museum, which provides poignant exhibits and information about the devastating effects of nuclear warfare. The park also houses the iconic A-Bomb Dome, a UNESCO World Heritage Site symbol of resilience and peace.

Miyajima Island. Just a short ferry ride from Hiroshima, Miyajima Island captivates visitors with its natural beauty and cultural treasures. The island's most famous landmark is the Itsukushima Shrine, known for its floating torii gate, which appears suspended in the water during high tide. Stroll through the island's charming streets, interact with friendly deer, and savor local delicacies like Momiji manju, a maple leaf-shaped sweet.

Hiroshima Castle. Immerse yourself in history at Hiroshima Castle, reconstructing the original 16th-century castle. Climb to the top of the castle tower for panoramic views of the city and learn about its samurai heritage through informative displays. Surrounding the castle is the tranquil Hiroshima Castle Park, offering a serene escape amidst cherry blossoms in the spring and vibrant foliage in the autumn.

Hiroshima Peace Memorial Ceremony. Pay your respects and witness the annual Hiroshima Peace Memorial Ceremony on August 6th, the anniversary of the atomic bombing. This solemn event brings people together worldwide to honor the victims, promote peace, and advocate for a world free of nuclear weapons.

Shukkeien Garden. Step into a serene oasis at Shukkeien Garden, a traditional Japanese garden in Hiroshima. Discover meticulously manicured landscapes, tea houses, a central pond, and various scenic viewpoints. This tranquil retreat is particularly stunning during cherry blossom season and offers a peaceful respite from the city's bustling streets.

Itsukushima Shrine. While visiting Miyajima Island, don't miss the opportunity to explore the iconic Itsukushima Shrine. Admire the stunning architecture, stroll through the picturesque grounds, and experience the magical atmosphere of this UNESCO World Heritage Site.

Hiroshima Museum of Art. Engage with the vibrant art scene of Hiroshima at the Hiroshima Museum of Art. The museum showcases a diverse collection of Japanese and Western art, including works by renowned artists. Enjoy temporary exhibitions and gain insights into the local art scene and cultural expressions.

Mazda Museum. For automobile enthusiasts, a visit to the Mazda Museum is a must. Learn about the history and innovation of Mazda automobiles through interactive displays and exhibits. Discover the company's technological advancements and explore its collection of iconic vehicles.

Hiroshima City Manga Library. Dive into the world of manga at the Hiroshima City Manga Library, a haven for manga lovers. Browse through a vast collection of manga titles, relax in the cozy reading areas, and learn about the impact of manga on Japanese culture and society.

Hiroshima Orizuru Tower. Gain a bird's-eye view of Hiroshima from the Hiroshima Orizuru Tower, a modern observation deck offering panoramic cityscape vistas. Enjoy stunning views of the Peace Memorial Park, the A-Bomb Dome, and the surrounding mountains. Learn about the significance of origami cranes and participate in folding paper cranes, a symbol of peace and hope.

KAMAKURA

Great Buddha of Kamakura. The Great Buddha, or Daibutsu, is a towering bronze statue in Kamakura. This iconic landmark is a must-visit attraction, representing the city's rich history and cultural heritage. Marvel at the sheer size and craftsmanship of the statue, which dates back to the 13th century, and explore the serene surroundings of Kotokuin Temple.

Tsurugaoka Hachimangu Shrine. Immerse yourself in the spiritual atmosphere of Kamakura at Tsurugaoka Hachimangu Shrine. This prominent Shinto shrine is dedicated to Hachiman, the god of war and the patron deity of the samurai. Admire the impressive main hall, stroll through the wooded pathways, and witness traditional ceremonies if you're lucky. The shrine's location at the base of the city's central hill provides a picturesque setting.

Enoshima Island. Just a short walk across the Kamakura connecting bridge, Enoshima Island offers a delightful escape from the city. Explore the island's picturesque landscapes, visit the Enoshima Shrine, and enjoy panoramic coastline views from the Enoshima Sea Candle observation tower. The island is also known for its beautiful beaches, making it a popular destination for swimmers and surfers during the summer months.

Hokokuji Temple (Bamboo Temple). Seek tranquility and natural beauty at Hokokuji Temple, often called the Bamboo Temple. This Zen Buddhist temple is renowned for its bamboo grove, creating a serene and peaceful atmosphere. Take a meditative stroll through the bamboo forest, visit the teahouse to enjoy a traditional matcha tea, and explore the temple's exquisite gardens.

Kamakura's Coastal Walk. Embark on a scenic coastal walk in Kamakura, starting from Yuigahama Beach and following the picturesque coastline. Enjoy breathtaking sea views, visit quaint residential areas, and discover hidden gems. The coastal walk offers a different perspective of Kamakura, allowing you to appreciate its natural beauty and relaxed atmosphere.

There's no question that Japan offers many tourist opportunities for every level of traveler in Japan. From sites rich in centuries of history to architectural buildings that seem to touch the sky, bustling shopping districts, and serene, peaceful parks. There is something for everyone to see, feel, and experience in this great country, and the Japanese people are more than welcoming to every tourist who chooses to spend just a bit of time in wanderlust and experience their country as they would like us to do.

THE SNOWY WONDERLAND OF JAPAN

ALTHOUGH NONE of our travel party was considering this adventure to include a visit to the unmatched skiing terrain in Japan, the country has a world where winter reigns supreme and where the mountains are draped in a sparkling white blanket that calls out to adventurers and snow enthusiasts alike. Nestled in the Land of the Rising Sun lies a winter wonderland where the magic of skiing transcends imagination. In this chapter, we invite you to discover the regions of Japan that boast an astonishing number of ski resorts, each with its unique charm and abundant snowfall. Brace yourself for a thrilling journey through snow-covered peaks and captivating landscapes as we explore the seasons and snowfall amounts that make Japan a paradise for winter sports.

HOKKAIDO PREFECTURE

One of Japan's most renowned ski regions is Hokkaido, a vast island in the country's northernmost reaches. Blessed with consistent snowfall and breathtaking mountain ranges, Hokkaido offers an extended ski season that typically begins in late November and lasts until early May. Resorts such as Niseko, Rusutsu, and Furano attract skiers from around the globe, offering a blend of powder snow and awe-inspiring landscapes. Hokkaido sets the stage for unforgettable winter adventures with an average snowfall of over 15 meters (50 feet) each season.

Niseko. Widely regarded as one of the top ski resorts in Hokkaido and the world, Niseko offers an unparalleled skiing experience. Located on the slopes of Mount Niseko-Annupuri, the resort is famous for its abundant, high-quality powder snow. Niseko boasts a unique microclimate that consistently delivers impressive snowfall throughout the season, attracting avid skiers and snowboarders from around the globe. With interconnected resorts, including Niseko Village, Grand Hirafu, and Annupuri, Niseko provides diverse terrain suitable for all skill levels. Beyond the slopes, visitors can also enjoy the vibrant après-ski scene, natural hot springs (onsen), and various international dining options.

Elevation: 300 meters (984 feet) to 1,308 meters (4,291 feet)

Number of ski runs: Over 60 ski runs across the interconnected resorts

Notable features: Abundant, high-quality powder snow attracting skiers worldwide. Vibrant après-ski scene and international dining options. Natural hot springs (onsen) for relaxation after a day on the slopes

Rusutsu Resort. Nestled in the southwestern part of Hokkaido, Rusutsu Resort is a winter paradise offering an abundance of snow and diverse terrain. The resort features three interconnected mountains—West Mountain, East Mountain, and Mount Isola—providing skiers and snowboarders with over 42 kilometers (26 miles) of slopes to explore. Rusutsu is known for its family-friendly atmosphere, with a wide range of activities for all ages, including snow parks, tubing, and an indoor amusement park. The resort's breathtaking scenery and panoramic views of Mount Yotei add to its allure.

Elevation: 400 meters (1,312 feet) to 994 meters (3,261 feet)

Number of ski runs: Over 42 kilometers (26 miles) of slopes

Notable features: Three interconnected mountains offering a diverse range of terrain. Family-friendly atmosphere with activities such as snow parks and tubing. Breathtaking views of Mount Yotei and a charming winter ambiance

Furano. Situated in central Hokkaido, Furano captures the essence of a traditional Japanese ski town while offering exceptional skiing opportunities. Famous for its consistently dry powder snow, Furano Resort features two main mountains, Furano Zone and Kitanomine Zone, each with a unique charm. The resort caters to skiers and snowboarders of all levels, with a good balance of gentle slopes for beginners and challenging runs for advanced riders. Beyond skiing, visitors can explore the picturesque town, indulge in local cuisine, and soak in the revitalizing hot springs after a day on the slopes.

Elevation: 235 meters (771 feet) to 1,120 meters (3,675 feet)

Number of ski runs: 28 runs across the Furano and Kitanomine zones

Notable features: Consistently dry powder snow for exceptional skiing conditions. A balanced mix of slopes that is suitable for beginners and advanced riders. Quaint traditional Japanese ski town with local cuisine and rejuvenating hot springs

These three ski resorts in Hokkaido showcase the region's exceptional snow quality, stunning natural landscapes, and warm hospitality that has made skiing in Japan a sought-after experience. Whether you seek thrilling slopes, picturesque surroundings, or a blend of outdoor adventure and cultural immersion, Hokkaido's ski resorts offer an unforgettable winter getaway.

NAGANO PREFECTURE

Traveling southward, the Nagano Prefecture captures the essence of traditional Japan while boasting world-class ski resorts. This region, renowned for hosting the 1998 Winter Olympics, is home to iconic destinations like Hakuba, Nozawa Onsen, and Shiga Kogen. Nagano experiences a long winter season, typically starting mid-December and lasting until early April. The snowfall here is abundant, with an average annual accumulation of around 10 meters (33 feet). This picturesque region, surrounded by the majestic Japanese Alps, offers skiers and snowboarders a diverse range of slopes and terrain to suit all levels of expertise.

> **Hakuba.** Hakuba is a world-renowned ski destination located in the northern part of Nagano. It has several interconnected ski resorts, including Happo-One, Goryu, and Hakuba 47. The region gained international recognition by hosting several events during the 1998 Winter Olympics. Hakuba offers a variety of terrain suitable for all levels, from gentle slopes for beginners to challenging steeps for advanced skiers and snowboarders. With its stunning backdrop of the Japanese Alps, Hakuba provides breathtaking views, excellent snow conditions, and a vibrant après-ski scene.

Elevation: Depending on the specific resort within Hakuba Valley, ranging from around 700 meters (2,297 feet) to over 1,800 meters (5,906 feet).

Number of ski runs: Hakuba Valley comprises multiple resorts with over 200 ski runs.

Notable features: Diverse terrain suitable for all skill levels, including steep slopes and backcountry areas. Hosted various events during the 1998 Winter Olympics, leaving a legacy of well-maintained infrastructure. Stunning views of the Japanese Alps and the iconic snow-covered peaks.

Nozawa Onsen. Nestled in the northern part of Nagano, Nozawa Onsen combines traditional Japanese charm with fantastic skiing opportunities. This picturesque village is famous for its natural hot springs (onsen) and preserved Edo-period streets. The ski resort itself offers a range of slopes catering to different abilities, from gentle groomers to thrilling tree runs. Nozawa Onsen boasts a reliable snowfall, ensuring excellent conditions throughout the winter season. After a day on the slopes, visitors can indulge in the village's renowned hot springs and savor authentic Japanese cuisine.

Elevation: The village sits at an elevation of approximately 565 meters (1,854 feet), with ski runs reaching up to 1,650 meters (5,413 feet).

The number of ski runs: Over 36 kilometers (22 miles) of ski runs, catering to different abilities.

Notable features: Famous for its abundant natural hot springs (onsen), offering a rejuvenating experience after a day on the slopes. Traditional charm with wooden ryokan inns, narrow streets, and a vibrant local atmosphere. The long ski season and reliable snowfall make it an ideal destination for skiing and cultural immersion.

Shiga Kogen. As the largest ski resort in Japan, Shiga Kogen offers an expansive winter playground within the Joshinetsu Kogen National Park. This vast ski area encompasses interconnected resorts, including Yokoteyama, Ichinose, and Okushiga Kogen. Shiga Kogen hosted various alpine skiing events during the 1998 Winter Olympics. Shiga Kogen caters to all skill levels with a wide range of slopes, from gentle beginner runs to challenging black diamonds. The resort's high elevation ensures abundant snowfall, providing excellent powder conditions throughout the season. Skiing amidst the serene beauty of Shiga Kogen's alpine landscapes is a truly unforgettable experience.

Elevation: Ranging from around 1,300 meters (4,265 feet) to 2,307 meters (7,570 feet).

Number of ski runs: Over 80 ski runs spread across 18 interconnected ski areas.

Notable features: Hosted various alpine skiing events during the 1998 Winter Olympics, showcasing its exceptional terrain. Abundance of natural snowfall throughout the season, making it a favorite destination for powder enthusiasts. Panoramic views of the surrounding mountains, including the iconic active volcano, Mount Yake.

These ski resorts in Nagano; Hakuba, Nozawa Onsen, and Shiga Kogen, offer the region a wide array of skiing opportunities, stunning natural scenery, and cultural attractions. Each resort offers a unique experience, from Hakuba's Olympic legacy to Nozawa Onsen's traditional hot spring village charm and Shiga Kogen's vast interconnected slopes. Whether you're seeking thrilling runs, traditional Japanese ambiance, or simply the joy of gliding down snow-covered mountains, Nagano's ski resorts have something special to offer.

HONSHU REGION

Moving to the main island of Honshu, we find the Tohoku region, encompassing areas such as Yamagata, Akita, and Aomori. Blessed with heavy snowfall thanks to its proximity to the Sea of Japan, Tohoku's ski season typically begins in December and stretches through to late March. Resorts like Zao Onsen, Gala Yuzawa, and Myoko Kogen showcase the region's unique winter landscapes, where snow-covered trees create an otherworldly spectacle known as "snow monsters." With an average snowfall of around 8 to 10 meters (26 to 33 feet) each season, Tohoku promises an unforgettable winter experience.

> **Myoko Kogen.** Located in Niigata Prefecture, Myoko Kogen is renowned for its abundant snowfall and picturesque mountain landscapes. The resort consists of several interconnected ski areas, including Akakura Onsen, Suginohara, and Ikenotaira Onsen. Myoko Kogen offers a variety of terrain suitable for all skill levels, with a combination of groomed runs, tree skiing, and backcountry options. With an average snowfall of over 14 meters (46 feet) each season, Myoko Kogen provides excellent powder conditions and breathtaking views of Mount Myoko. The region also boasts a rich cultural heritage and relaxing hot spring baths.
>
> Elevation: Varies within the resort, ranging from approximately 400 meters (1,312 feet) to 2,454 meters (8,051 feet).
>
> Typical number of ski runs: Myoko Kogen offers over 80 ski runs spread across its interconnected ski areas.

Notable features: Abundant snowfall, averaging over 14 meters (46 feet) per season, providing excellent powder conditions. Diverse terrain suitable for all skill levels, including groomed runs, tree skiing, and backcountry options. Breathtaking views of Mount Myoko and the surrounding mountain ranges, adding to the scenic appeal.

Zao Onsen. Situated in Yamagata Prefecture, Zao Onsen is known for its unique "snow monsters" (juhyo) formed by the accumulation of snow and ice on the trees. This phenomenon creates a stunning and otherworldly winter landscape. Zao Onsen offers a wide range of ski runs, including both beginner-friendly slopes and challenging expert trails. The resort's famous "Sky Cable" gondola provides access to panoramic views and opportunities for backcountry skiing. In addition to skiing, visitors can explore the traditional hot spring town of Zao Onsen and indulge in local cuisine.

Elevation: Ranges from approximately 800 meters (2,625 feet) to 1,660 meters (5,446 feet) at the peak.

Typical number of ski runs: Zao Onsen boasts over 40 ski runs catering to various abilities.

Notable features: Unique "snow monsters" (juhyo) created by the accumulation of snow and ice on trees, creating a stunning winter landscape. A wide range of skiing options, including beginner-friendly slopes and challenging expert trails. The "Sky Cable" gondola provides access to panoramic views and opportunities for backcountry skiing.

Gala Yuzawa. Gala Yuzawa stands out as one of Japan's most accessible ski resorts, located just 75 minutes from Tokyo by bullet train. This convenience makes it an ideal day trip destination for visitors staying in the capital. Gala Yuzawa features a central station directly connected to the ski slopes, eliminating the need for transportation between the resort and train station. The resort offers a wide range of ski runs catering to all skill levels, from gentle beginner slopes to challenging black diamond trails. With a range of facilities, including rental shops, restaurants, and hot springs, Gala Yuzawa provides a complete skiing experience within easy reach of Tokyo.

Elevation: Approximately 800 meters (2,625 feet).

Typical number of ski runs: Gala Yuzawa offers around 17 ski runs across its interconnected ski area.

Notable features: Convenient access from Tokyo, located just 75 minutes away by bullet train, making it an accessible day trip destination.The resort features a central station directly connected to the ski slopes, eliminating the need for transportation between the resort and train station. A range of facilities, including rental shops, restaurants, and hot springs, providing a complete skiing experience.

These three notable ski resorts in Honshu; Myoko Kogen, Zao Onsen, and Gala Yuzawa, offer diverse skiing opportunities, stunning winter landscapes, and unique features. Whether you're seeking powder-filled slopes, enchanting snow formations, or convenient access from Tokyo, these resorts showcase the best of skiing in Honshu. Enjoy carving down the slopes, immersing yourself in local traditions, and experiencing the natural beauty of Japan's main island.

As you traverse Japan's ski regions, you'll encounter varying climates, terrain, and cultural experiences. Each region offers its unique blend of winter sports thrills from the powdery slopes of Hokkaido to the enchanting winter landscapes of Nagano, Tohoku, and the Japan Alps. So, prepare to carve through pristine powder, immerse yourself in vibrant snow festivals, and indulge in the warm hospitality that defines Japan's ski resorts. Whether you're a seasoned enthusiast or a first-time visitor to the world of Japanese snow sports, Japan's winter wonderland eagerly awaits your arrival.

WINTER FESTIVALS

As winter blankets the landscapes of Hokkaido, Nagano, Tohoku, and the Japan Alps, a vibrant tapestry of winter festivals emerges, capturing the hearts of locals and drawing visitors from far and wide. Each region boasts its own unique celebration, showcasing the artistic prowess of snow and ice sculptors, the fiery energy of traditional rituals, and the enchanting beauty of illuminated landscapes. From the world-renowned Sapporo Snow Festival in Hokkaido, where towering snow sculptures captivate millions, to the mesmerizing spectacle of the Takayama Winter Festival in the Japan Alps, where illuminated floats parade through snow-covered streets, these winter festivals are a testament to Japan's rich cultural heritage and the enduring allure of its winter wonderland. Whether it's witnessing the mystical snow monsters of Zao Onsen or immersing oneself in the warm glow of lantern-lit snow lanterns in Hirosaki, these festivals offer an array of unforgettable experiences, weaving together tradition, artistry, and the magic of winter in Japan.

Hokkaido

Sapporo Snow Festival (Sapporo): One of Japan's most famous winter festivals, the Sapporo Snow Festival showcases enormous snow and ice sculptures. The festival attracts millions of visitors each year who marvel at the intricate and grand creations, including replicas of famous landmarks, characters, and fantastical sculptures.

Otaru Snow Light Path Festival (Otaru): The Otaru Snow Light Path Festival transforms the historic town of Otaru into a magical winter wonderland. The festival features beautifully illuminated snow sculptures and lantern displays along the canal and in the streets, creating a romantic and enchanting atmosphere.

Nagano

Nozawa Onsen Fire Festival (Nozawa Onsen): The Nozawa Onsen Fire Festival is a vibrant and energetic event held annually to pray for a plentiful harvest and good health. Locals dressed in traditional attire carry giant torches through the streets, culminating in a fiery spectacle where a massive wooden shrine is set ablaze, accompanied by music, dancing, and fireworks.

Matsumoto Castle Ice Sculpture Festival (Matsumoto): The Matsumoto Castle Ice Sculpture Festival takes place in the grounds of the iconic Matsumoto Castle. The festival showcases impressive ice sculptures depicting historical figures, mythical creatures, and famous landmarks. Visitors can explore the castle grounds at night, marveling at the illuminated sculptures.

Tohuku

Hirosaki Castle Snow Lantern Festival (Hirosaki): The Hirosaki Castle Snow Lantern Festival is held in the grounds of Hirosaki Castle, where the snow-covered landscape is adorned with hundreds of beautifully crafted snow lanterns. Visitors can enjoy the magical atmosphere, stroll through the illuminated castle grounds, and witness captivating performances and traditional music.

Zao Snow Monster Festival (Yamagata): The Zao Snow Monster Festival celebrates the unique "snow monsters" (juhyo) formed by the accumulation of snow and ice on the trees in Zao Onsen. The festival features illuminated snow monsters, snow slides, and various events such as traditional performances, snowball fights, and fireworks.

Japan Alps

Takayama Winter Festival (Takayama): The Takayama Winter Festival is a spectacular event held in the historic town of Takayama. The festival showcases elaborately crafted floats (yatai) illuminated with lanterns paraded through the streets. The highlight is the night procession, where the floats are pulled through the snow-covered town, accompanied by traditional music and performances.

Shirakawa-go Winter Light-Up (Shirakawa-go): The Shirakawa-go Winter Light-Up is a magical event where the traditional thatched-roof houses of Shirakawa-go village are illuminated, creating a fairytale-like ambiance. Visitors can wander through the village, enjoying the picturesque scenery and the warm glow of the illuminated houses against the snowy backdrop.

These winter festivals not only provide visual delights but also immerse visitors in the cultural tapestry of Japan. They serve as a reminder of the country's deep-rooted traditions and the importance of community and celebration. The festivals become a platform for locals to showcase their craftsmanship, culinary expertise, and artistic expressions, creating a sense of pride and unity among the participants. The festivals vividly depict Japan's cultural richness, from the rhythmic beats of traditional drums to the vibrant colors of intricately designed floats.

Beyond the visual and cultural experiences, these festivals offer a chance to engage with the local communities and embrace the warm hospitality of the regions. Visitors can indulge in traditional winter delicacies like hot pots, grilled seafood, and steaming bowls of ramen, savoring the flavors unique to each locality. They can also partake in activities such as snow sports, winter hiking, and traditional ceremonies, immersing themselves in the dynamic spirit of the season.

As you've read, the winter festivals in Hokkaido, Nagano, Tohoku, and the Japan Alps capture the essence of Japan's snowy delights, inviting travelers to experience the magic of winter in a truly extraordinary way. Whether it's the awe-inspiring snow sculptures, the ancient rituals passed down through generations, or the stunning displays of illuminated landscapes, these festivals weave together tradition, artistry, and the sheer joy of embracing winter's embrace. As visitors immerse themselves in the festivities, they become part of a cherished tradition, creating lasting memories and forging connections that transcend language and cultural barriers.

10

FINAL THOUGHTS

As we come to the end of this journey through the captivating country of Japan, we hope that you have gained valuable knowledge, insightful perspectives, and practical tips that will enhance your experience as you embark on your adventure to this remarkable country overflowing with history. Throughout these chapters, we have touched on the many parts of planning your trip, understanding the efficient rail system, navigating bustling Haneda Airport, and immersing yourself in the art of dining in Japanese style.

We have explored five amazing cities, each with distinct charm and allure. From the vibrant metropolis of Tokyo, with its skyscrapers and neon-lit streets, to the cultural and historical treasure troves of Kyoto and Hiroshima, Japan has offered us a variety of contrasting experiences. Along the way, we have uncovered the secrets of finding comfortable lodging, gaining insights into the local weather patterns, and discovering the top attractions showcasing this captivating nation's rich heritage and natural beauty.

We have also unveiled the snowy wonderland nestled within Japan's mountainous regions. The allure of pristine powder snow, awe-inspiring ski resorts, and the sheer excitement of winter sports beckons those seeking an exhilarating and unforgettable experience. The enchanting ski regions of Hokkaido, Nagano, and other parts of Honshu offer a paradise for snow enthusiasts, where the beauty of nature merges seamlessly with the thrill of adventure.

As you embark on your own expedition to Japan, armed with the knowledge and insights gained from these pages, we sincerely hope your trip is filled with delightful surprises, memorable encounters, and a deep appreciation for the unique blend of tradition and modernity that defines this extraordinary country. Experiencing the vibrant energy of Tokyo's bustling streets, savoring the flavors of Osaka's vibrant food scene, marveling at Kyoto's ancient temples, reflecting upon the resilience of Hiroshima, and immersing yourself in Japan's snowy landscapes are just waiting for your arrival.

From the bustling cities to the tranquil mountains, Japan invites you to embark on a journey that will captivate your senses, broaden your horizons, and leave an indelible mark on your heart. May your travels be filled with joy, discovery, and a deep connection to the wonders of this fascinating land.

Safe travels and a warm *Konnichiwa!* to your planning and your unforgettable adventure in Japan.

Wishing you a safe and wonderful trip to Japan!

~ P.D. Mason

Help Spread the Word To Fellow Travelers!

There's an amazing adventure ahead of you, and you're just at the start of it. This is your chance to help someone else discover everything Japan has to offer through the simplicity of using "Travel Japan" as the roadmap to crafting their own individual itinerary.

By sharing your honest opinion of this book on Amazon and a little about what you found inside, you will help other people in their own stages of Japan travel planning to find the essential guidance they might not have found otherwise.

I humbly thank you so much for your support. Your role is vital, and I appreciate your support tremendously.

Scan the QR code to leave your review on Amazon.

ABOUT THE AUTHOR

Paul "P.D." Mason lives in the upper Midwest region of the United States with his wife and his trusted writing companion, a knee-high pit bull terrier mix named Sugar. Paul is an independent author writing for SugarDog Publishing and has written multiple fiction and non-fiction books on various topics and fictional storylines that resonate with his readers.

ALSO BY P.D. MASON

Financially Smart Career Planning For Teens: The Roadmap to Making Informed Decisions In An Uncertain Job Market, Prevent Feeling Overwhelmed & Analysis Paralysis To Achieve Affordable College Degrees(2023, SugarDog Publishing)

Apprenticeship Career Planning for Teens: A Comprehensive Guide to Securing Apprenticeships in High Demand Industries Without Taking on Years of College Debt (2023, SugarDog Publishing)

Skilled Trade Career Planning For Teens: The Handbook Of Lucrative Skilled Trades & High Paying Occupations That Don't Require Expensive College Degrees (2023, SugarDog Publishing)

8 Simple Techniques For Easy Kitchen Knife Sharpening: Keep Your Home Kitchen Knives Sharp Using Trusted Tools, Methods & Techniques Taught By Professionals! (2023, SugarDog Publishing)

Construction Project Management 101: For Beginners & New Graduates 2024 Student Edition (2023, SugarDog Publishing)

REFERENCES

18 Best Temples and Shrines in Kyoto - Go Guides. (2021). Hotels.com. https://www.hotels.com/go/japan/best-kyoto-temples

Alyse. (2023, June 1). *Fun Things to Do in Hiroshima & Meaningful Attractions*. The Invisible Tourist. https://www.theinvisibletourist.com/things-to-do-in-hiroshima-attractions/

Atomic Bomb Dome. (n.d.). The Official Guide to Hiroshima | Dive! Hiroshima. Retrieved June 8, 2023, from https://dive-hiroshima.com/en/feature/world-heritage-dome/

Bache, B. (2023, March 31). *Osaka: A City Rich in History and Culture - Sakuraco*. Sakuraco. https://sakura.co/blog/osaka-history-and-culture/

Baker, F. (2022, October 24). *Japanese Dining Etiquette and Table Manners*. Bokksu. https://www.bokksu.com/blogs/news/dining-etiquette-in-japan

Blog, J. W. T. (2021, September 23). *12 Original Castles in Japan*. Japan Wonder Travel Blog. https://blog.japanwondertravel.com/12-original-castles-in-japan-19497

Bureau, T. C. & V. (2022, October 19). *Ginza*. The Official Tokyo Travel Guide, GO TOKYO. https://www.gotokyo.org/en/destinations/central-tokyo/ginza/index.html

Bureau, T. C. & V. (2023, February 1). *Haneda Airport*. The Official Tokyo Travel Guide, GO TOKYO. https://www.gotokyo.org/en/plan/airport-access/haneda-airport/index.html

Cheapo, T. (n.d.). *101 Cheap and Free Things to Do in Tokyo | Tokyo Cheapo*. Https://Tokyocheapo.com/. https://tokyocheapo.com/entertainment/101-free-and-cheap-things-to-do-in-tokyo/

D., A. (2022, April 28). *Top 38 Most Beautiful Shrines and Temples in Japan*. Top 38 Most Beautiful Shrines and Temples in Japan. https://gowithguide.com/blog/top-38-most-beautiful-shrines-and-temples-in-japan-1873

Davidson, L. (2021, September 16). *Osaka Castle*. History Hit. https://www.historyhit.com/locations/osaka-castle/

Enoshima. (2023, February 11). Wikipedia. https://en.wikipedia.org/wiki/Enoshima

Enoshima Sea Candle. (2023, January 12). Wikipedia. https://en.wikipedia.org/wiki/Enoshima_Sea_Candle

Greuner, T. (2021, March 16). *The most beautiful Starbucks in Japan*. Time out Tokyo. https://www.timeout.com/tokyo/restaurants/the-most-beautiful-starbucks-in-japan

120 | REFERENCES

Greuner, T., & Furutani, K. (2022, September 29). *33 of the best free things to do in Tokyo*. Time out Tokyo. https://www.timeout.com/tokyo/things-to-do/30-free-things-to-do-in-tokyo

Hays, J. (n.d.). *OSAKA: ITS HISTORY, PEOPLE AND ECONOMY | Facts and Details*. Factsanddetails.com. https://factsanddetails.com/japan/cat25/sub-168/item981.html

Hiroshima Travel Guide - What to do in Hiroshima. (2019, April 16). Japan-Guide.com. https://www.japan-guide.com/e/e2160.html

https://www.facebook.com/aworldinreach. (2020, January 24). *Free Things to Do in Kyoto, Japan*. A World in Reach. https://www.aworldinreach.com/free-things-to-do-in-kyoto/

Japan-guide.com. (2018, April 17). *Shinto Shrines*. Japan-Guide.com. https://www.japan-guide.com/e/e2059.html

Japan-guide.com. (2019, June 30). *Japanese Table Manners*. Japan-Guide.com. https://www.japan-guide.com/e/e2005.html

japan-guide.com. (2019). *Osaka Travel: Osaka Castle (Osakajo)*. Japan-Guide.com. https://www.japan-guide.com/e/e4000.html

JR EAST Travel Service Center (Narita) | Customer Support | JR-EAST. (n.d.). Www.jreast.co.jp. Retrieved June 22, 2023, from https://www.jreast.co.jp/e/customer_support/service_center.html

Kagami, L. (2021, July 29). *Kyoto: The City of Shrines and Temples*. LEN Journeys. https://lenjourneys.com/kyoto-the-city-of-shrines-and-temples/

Kamakura Travel Guide - What to do in Kamakura. (2000). Japan-Guide.com. https://www.japan-guide.com/e/e2166.html

L., R. (2022, November 28). *The 20 Most Beautiful Shrines and Temples in Kyoto*. The 20 Most Beautiful Shrines and Temples in Kyoto. https://gowithguide.com/blog/the-20-most-beautiful-shrines-and-temples-in-kyoto-1914

lasma.plone. (2023, April 29). *18 Best Free Things to Do in Kyoto + Kyoto Budget Tips*. Lasma Plone. https://lasmaplone.com/free-things-to-do-in-kyoto/

Logan. (2016, July 29). *10 Unique Japanese Eating Etiquette Rules -*. Nomiyarestaurant.com. http://nomiyarestaurant.com/10-japanese-eating-etiquette-rules/

LTD, T. P. (n.d.). *TABLEALL - Access To Exclusive Restaurants In Japan*. TABLEALL. Retrieved June 22, 2023, from https://www.tableall.com/restaurants/area/Tokyo

Noho_B_M. (2017, December 26). *20 Best Restaurants in Tokyo 2021*. JapanWeb Magazine. https://jw-webmagazine.com/top-10-restaurants-in-tokyo-84d7716e963e/

Osaka - New World Encyclopedia. (n.d.). Www.newworldencyclopedia.org. https://www.newworldencyclopedia.org/entry/Osaka

Osaka Castle - OSAKA | IS JAPAN COOL? (n.d.). Osaka Castle - OSAKA | IS

REFERENCES | 121

JAPAN COOL? https://www.ana-cooljapan.com/destinations/osaka/osakacastle

Procedures of Passenger Clearance : Japan Customs. (n.d.). Www.customs.go.jp. https://www.customs.go.jp/english/summary/passenger.htm

Ski Resorts In Japan - Skiing in Japan. (n.d.). SkiJapan.com. Retrieved June 22, 2023, from https://www.skijapan.com/resorts/

The 30 best free attractions in Hiroshima. (n.d.). Wanderlog. Retrieved June 22, 2023, from https://wanderlog.com/list/geoCategory/129627/best-free-attractions-in-hiroshima

Tokyo Haneda Airport 5-Star Rating - Skytrax. (2019). Skytrax; Skytrax. https://skytraxratings.com/airports/tokyo-haneda-airport-rating

Tokyo Metropolitan Government Building Observatories. (n.d.). Tokyo Metropolitan Government. Retrieved June 8, 2023, from https://www.metro.tokyo.lg.jp/english/offices/observat.html

Tokyo Monorail : Monorail Guide > Haneda Airport Terminal 3 > Station Information. (n.d.). Www.tokyo-Monorail.co.jp. Retrieved June 22, 2023, from https://www.tokyo-monorail.co.jp/english/guidance/kokusaisen/index.html

TOKYO SKYTREE. (n.d.). Www.tokyo-Skytree.jp. Retrieved January 15, 2023, from https://www.tokyo-skytree.jp/en/

Varga, C. (2023 6). *Complete Guide to Fushimi Inari Shrine | You Could Travel.* Complete Guide to Fushimi Inari Shrine | You Could Travel. https://www.youcouldtravel.com/travel-blog/how-to-have-the-best-experience-at-fushimi-inari-shrine

Wikipedia Contributors. (2018, December 6). *Kamakura.* Wikipedia; Wikimedia Foundation. https://en.wikipedia.org/wiki/Kamakura

Wikipedia Contributors. (2019a, April 3). *List of Emperors of Japan.* Wikipedia; Wikimedia Foundation. https://en.wikipedia.org/wiki/List_of_Emperors_of_Japan

Wikipedia Contributors. (2019b, August 6). *Shinkansen.* Wikipedia; Wikimedia Foundation. https://en.wikipedia.org/wiki/Shinkansen

Wikipedia Contributors. (2019c, October 19). *Tokyo Imperial Palace.* Wikipedia; Wikimedia Foundation. https://en.wikipedia.org/wiki/Tokyo_Imperial_Palace

Wikipedia Contributors. (2019d, October 21). *Fushimi Inari-taisha.* Wikipedia; Wikimedia Foundation. https://en.wikipedia.org/wiki/Fushimi_Inari-taisha

Wikipedia Contributors. (2020, August 13). *Nijō Castle.* Wikipedia; Wikimedia Foundation. https://en.wikipedia.org/wiki/Nij%C5%8D_Castle

Made in the USA
Middletown, DE
08 April 2024

52763052R00076